# CONTENTS

## Chapter One: Ageing Trends

The ageing process   1

What is ageing?   2

Older people in the UK   3

Facts and figures: global ageing   5

10 facts on ageing and the life course   6

Profile of the UK's older people   7

Age discrimination   8

Number of working pensioners continues to rise   10

Knowledge of age laws increasing   11

Work experienced   12

Plans to outlaw age discrimination announced   13

Ignoring old age won't keep you young   14

Reinventing the retirement cliff edge   15

Dignified conclusions   16

Loneliness a major worry   17

Prevalence of elder abuse   18

## Chapter Two: The Cost of Ageing

Retirees spending freely   19

Life begins at 55   20

Aim high, save low   21

Next generation of Brits facing bleak future   22

Pensions Act 2007   23

Pension could protect world's poorest   24

UK state pension is 'worst in Europe'   25

Charging into poverty   26

Care homes   27

Huge public worries about quality of care   28

Funding long-term care   29

Out of sight, out of mind   30

## Chapter Three: Ageing and Health

Why do we age?   31

Why do we die?   32

Lounging around could speed up ageing process   33

Increasing life expectancy   34

Life expectancy and healthy ageing   34

What is dementia?   35

Who is affected by Alzheimer's disease?   36

Reversing the signs of Alzheimer's   37

Alzheimer's disease to quadruple by 2050   38

Fear of dementia   39

Seniors playground swings into action   39

Key Facts   40

Glossary   41

Index   42

Additional Resources   43

Acknowledgements   44

# Useful information for readers

Dear Reader,

## *Issues: An Ageing Population*

Medical advances mean we are all living longer; but with the percentage of the UK population who are over 65 predicted to rise by over 60% in the next 25 years, does society have the resources to cope with an ageing population? Older people are already at risk of fuel poverty and the cost of care in older age is prohibitive. Meanwhile, young people are not planning for older age and face an even bleaker future than their parents and grandparents. This book looks at the financial and social implications of an ageing population, covering issues such as the economics of ageing, isolation, elder abuse, care issues and health in older age.

## The purpose of *Issues*

**An Ageing Population** is the one hundred and fifty-ninth volume in the **Issues** series. The aim of this series is to offer up-to-date information about important issues in our world. Whether you are a regular reader or new to the series, we do hope you find this book a useful overview of the many and complex issues involved in the topic. This title replaces an older volume in the **Issues** series, Volume 105: **Ageing Issues,** which is now out of print.

Titles in the **Issues** series are resource books designed to be of especial use to those undertaking project work or requiring an overview of facts, opinions and information on a particular subject, particularly as a prelude to undertaking their own research.

The information in this book is not from a single author, publication or organisation; the value of this unique series lies in the fact that it presents information from a wide variety of sources, including:

⇨ Government reports and statistics
⇨ Newspaper articles and features
⇨ Information from think-tanks and policy institutes
⇨ Magazine features and surveys
⇨ Website material
⇨ Literature from lobby groups and charitable organisations.*

## Critical evaluation

Because the information reprinted here is from a number of different sources, readers should bear in mind the origin of the text and whether the source is likely to have a particular bias or agenda when presenting information (just as they would if undertaking their own research). It is hoped that, as you read about the many aspects of the issues explored in this book, you will critically evaluate the information presented. It is important that you decide whether you are being presented with facts or opinions. Does the writer give a biased or an unbiased report? If an opinion is being expressed, do you agree with the writer?

**An Ageing Population** offers a useful starting point for those who need convenient access to information about the many issues involved. However, it is only a starting point. Following each article is a URL to the relevant organisation's website, which you may wish to visit for further information.

Kind regards,

Lisa Firth
Editor, **Issues** series

*\* Please note that Independence Publishers has no political affiliations or opinions on the topics covered in the **Issues** series, and any views quoted in this book are not necessarily those of the publisher or its staff.*

# An Ageing Population

**ISSUES**

**Volume 159**

*Series Editor*

*Lisa Firth*

 *Independence*

Educational Publishers
Cambridge

First published by Independence
The Studio, High Green
Great Shelford
Cambridge CB22 5EG
England

© Independence 2008

## British Library Cataloguing in Publication Data

An Ageing Population – (Issues Series)
I. Firth, Lisa II. Series
362.6

ISBN 978 1 86168 452 3

## Printed in Great Britain

MWL Print Group Ltd

## Cover

The illustration on the front cover is by
Don Hatcher.

# The ageing process

## Information from Guide2care

One of the greatest current challenges in medical science is to understand the ageing process in sufficient detail to allow us to open new paths to improving the quality of the later years of life. It is important to be clear that the goal is to improve the quality of life in old age rather than to extend the length of life regardless of its quality. All of us, if we live long enough, will experience aspects of ageing that will increase our frailty and limit our independence but we do not all age in the same way. Some will remain free from disease for a very long time, whereas others will develop one or more of a range of age-related diseases.

## Current understanding of the ageing process places a priority on good nutrition

What is normal ageing and how is it related to the diseases of old age? Do different diseases share common causative mechanisms?

Can these diseases be slowed or prevented by changes in nutrition or lifestyle, as well as by medical drugs?

### What is ageing and why does it occur?

In one sense we all know what ageing is, although scientifically the mechanisms have been very hard to pin down. We used to think that ageing was programmed into us by some kind of death clock, but this view is no longer widely held. We now think that ageing happens because during our lifetime the cells and tissues of our bodies accumulate many microscopic faults that eventually get in the way of normal functions. The good news is that if we can find ways to reduce this damage, or to increase the effectiveness of our natural repair systems, we might delay the onset of disease.

### Cell ageing

Human cells from normal tissue can be propagated in the test tube, but eventually they stop growing, age and die. Cells grown from old donors divide less than cells from young donors, so there is good reason to believe that the study of cell ageing can throw light on the ageing of the body as a whole. Research is identifying some of the factors that appear to control cell ageing. The cells that make up the organs of the body (e.g. brain, skin, bone) age in different ways and at different rates. However, all cells have to cope with similar kinds of damage, and common factors may affect their ageing. Understanding the role of common factors in the development of different age-related diseases is a unique benefit that comes from studying the cellular basis of ageing. Work funded by Research into Ageing is examining how cells age. The kinds of damage most likely to cause ageing are in the genetic material (DNA) of cells and the accumulation of altered cellular components. Altered proteins are important in diseases as diverse as Alzheimer's disease and cataracts, while mutations play a part in cancers (many of which become commoner with age), and in muscle weakness. Much of the damage arises as a by-product of normal living. For example, 1-2% of the oxygen we breathe gives rise to highly reactive molecules called free radicals which can damage DNA and proteins. Our bodies have excellent natural protection against mutations and free radicals, which is why we live as long as we do, but some faults slip through.

### The role of genetics

Genetic research is providing valuable clues to ageing and age-related diseases. The fruit fly and soil nematode worm are helping to identify genes that affect life span. Many of these turn out to be genes

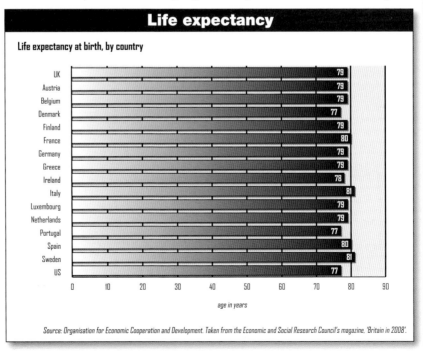

**Life expectancy**

Life expectancy at birth, by country

| Country | Age (years) |
|---|---|
| UK | 79 |
| Austria | 79 |
| Belgium | 79 |
| Denmark | 77 |
| Finland | 79 |
| France | 80 |
| Germany | 79 |
| Greece | 79 |
| Ireland | 78 |
| Italy | 81 |
| Luxembourg | 79 |
| Netherlands | 79 |
| Portugal | 77 |
| Spain | 80 |
| Sweden | 81 |
| US | 77 |

age in years

Source: Organisation for Economic Cooperation and Development. Taken from the Economic and Social Research Council's magazine, 'Britain in 2008'.

that control maintenance and repair systems. In humans, genes are being found that affect the risk of age-related diseases such as Alzheimer's disease and osteoarthritis.

### Nutrition and lifestyle

Current understanding of the ageing process places a priority on good nutrition, because food fuels the natural repair systems and provides the raw materials for healthy cell turnover. Low calorie intake in some animals has been shown to improve health in old age, but it is not known whether calorie restriction has the same effect in humans. Exercise has clear benefits for health, as long as precautions are taken to avoid injury. Recent work has shown that regular exercise can slow the development of age-related decline in muscle.

### The need for further research

Although much is known about the ageing process, we lack a detailed knowledge of the precise mechanisms and how these contribute to age-associated disease. Basic ageing research is a relatively new field. Not only do we still need answers to these fundamental questions, but we also need to train dedicated young researchers. Our goal is a deeper understanding of the mechanisms responsible for infirmity and disease in old age, which can be used to enhance and extend quality of life. The scale of the task is immense.

⇨ The above information is re-printed with kind permission from Guide2care. Visit www.guide2care. com for more information.

© Guide2care

# What is ageing?

## Information from The Naked Scientists

*Q: What is ageing? Is it caused by cumulative damage to cells as a result of everyday life or is it genetically programmed and if it is can we prevent it with, say, gene modification? (Questioned posed by Emily Stuart)*

A: It's both. Cells in the body are pre-programmed with a finite lifespan and a finite number of times that they can divide (split) to form daughter cells. For example, the red blood cells that carry oxygen to our tissues have a lifetime of 120 days after which they wear out and are broken down so that their constituents can be recycled. At the same time other cell types such as muscle and nerves can survive for much longer, even a lifetime, whilst the cells lining the mouth and intestines might last less than a day before being scraped off during a meal.

These cells are replaced by stem cells that divide (split) through the process of mitosis. However, scientists have found that every cell has a built-in limit on the number of times it can divide like this, known as the Hayflick number. This occurs because the ends of the DNA chromosomes contain structures called telomeres, which are similar in some ways to the piece of tape that protects the free ends of a shoelace. Whenever a cell divides a small amount of material is lost from each telomere. Eventually, after about thirty to forty cell divisions, the telomeres become too short and the cell can no longer divide. At this stage it's said to be senescent (aged).

Stem cells can also be forced into early senescence if their DNA becomes damaged. Switching the cell off like this is a protective mechanism to guard against cancer, which can occur when genetic changes (mutations) inappropriately activate a cell's growth systems.

This DNA damage is usually caused by reactive chemicals called free radicals that are produced by metabolism, by toxins we take into the body in things like cigarette smoke and by exposure to sunlight. Thankfully, vitamins and other anti-oxidants help to protect cells from the effects of radicals, which is why eating a healthy diet rich in antioxidants can help to slow down the ageing process.

Nevertheless, as we age the number of stem cells capable of producing new cells to repair damage, replace lost cells and react to infections steadily declines. This means that fewer resources are devoted to repair and growth causing tissues to steadily deteriorate, and that's why skin goes wrinkly!
*January 2008*

⇨ Information from Dr Chris Smith, The Naked Scientists. www. thenakedscientists.com.

© The Naked Scientists

-THERE'S A DOWNSIDE TO LIVING FOR EVER?!

IT'S NEVER AS GOOD AS THE FIRST 80 YEARS...

# Older people in the UK

## Information from Help the Aged

### Population

⇨ There are nearly 12 million pensioners, almost 1 in 5 of the UK's total population

⇨ There are 20.5 million people aged 50 years and over, over a third of the total UK population

⇨ There are 9,687,800 people in the UK aged 65 and above

⇨ About one and a quarter million people are aged 85 or over

⇨ There are eleven thousand centenarians

⇨ About 3.5 million older people (65+) live alone

### Population projections

⇨ The number of people aged 65 years and over is expected to rise by over 60% in the next 25 years to almost 15.8 million in 2031

⇨ The percentage of the total population who are over 65 is predicted to rise from 16% to over 22% in 2031 and nearly 26% in 2071

⇨ The number of people over 85 in the UK is predicted to have doubled in the next 25 years and to have trebled in the next 35

⇨ The population over 75 is projected to almost double in the next 30 years

### Life expectancy

⇨ Current life expectancy aged 65 is 84.7 for women and 81.9 for men. At birth, they are 81.3 and 76.9 respectively

⇨ Projections for 2025 for life expectancy at 65 are 87.5 for women and 85.1 for men

⇨ A female born in Glasgow City can expect to live 10.2 years less than one born in Kensington and Chelsea. For males, the difference is 12.6 years. The gaps are greater than they were for the previous year

⇨ The United Kingdom had a lower healthy life expectancy at birth (for males and females) and a smaller percentage of life expectancy without disability than the average of the 15 European Union countries in 2003

### Poverty and fuel poverty

⇨ 2.5 million pensioners (over one in five pensioners in the UK) live below the poverty line. (£151 for single pensioners and £226 for a couple)

⇨ Up to £5 billion of means-tested benefits that should rightfully go to older people in GB is unclaimed each year

⇨ For single pensioners mainly reliant on state pension, average disposable weekly income is £150

⇨ 15% of pensioners are in persistent poverty (below the poverty line for at least 3 out of the last 4 years in GB)

⇨ About 1.5 million pensioner households in the UK live in fuel poverty

### Income

⇨ In 2008/9, the full Basic State Pension is £90.70 for single pensioners and £145.05 for pensioner couples

⇨ The UK spends about 5% of its Gross Domestic Product on pension benefits, less than most other European countries

⇨ 1.3 million pensioners in the UK have no source of income other than the state pension and benefits

### Loneliness

⇨ Half of all people aged 75 and over live alone (the figure has reached 50% for the first time since the year 2000)

⇨ Over 1.2 million older people (13%) in the UK always or often feel lonely

⇨ 36% of people aged 65 and over in the UK feel out of touch with the pace of modern life and 9% say they feel cut off from society

⇨ Nearly half of all older people (about 4.6 million) consider the television as their main form of company

⇨ Over 1 million older people spent Christmas Day alone in 2004

### Isolation

⇨ 12% of older people (over 1.1 million) feel trapped in their own home

⇨ 7% of older people (nearly 700,000) don't go out more than once a week

⇨ 3% of older people never go out

⇨ 17% of older people have less than weekly contact with family, friends and neighbours

⇨ 11% have less than monthly contact

### Leisure

⇨ 9% of 65- to 74-year-olds and only 7% of those aged 75+ currently take part in learning

⇨ Only 29% of people aged 65 and over have ever used the internet

⇨ 50% of those aged 65-74 and 38% of those aged 75+ have taken part in some form of volunteering in the last 12 months. The average for all ages is 50%

⇨ People aged 65 and over spend on average three and three-quarters hours a day watching TV (or DVD/Video)

### Crime

⇨ 8% of people aged 60+ in England and Wales say they live in fear of crime

⇨ As an age group, the 75+ group is least likely to have a high level worry about burglary, car crime and violent crime. 65-74 is also less likely than the average to have a high level of worry about burglary and violent crime

⇨ Older people (especially those aged 65-74) are most likely to feel that crime is increasing 'a lot' in the country as a whole. However, older people are no more likely to perceive a similar increase of crime at a local level

## Housing and homelessness

⇨ 33% of the homes occupied by older people in England fail the decent homes standard (approximately 1.8 million households)

⇨ It is estimated that up to 42,000 older people are unofficially homeless in England and Wales

## Age discrimination

⇨ 73% of older people in Great Britain agree that age discrimination exists in the daily lives of older people

⇨ 68% of adults agree that once you reach very old age, people tend to treat you as a child

⇨ 95% of annual travel insurance policies impose an upper age limit

⇨ People aged 55-64 are twice as likely to be made redundant in organisational restructuring and reshaping exercises

⇨ Non-employment amongst people aged 50-69 could be costing the economy nearly £30 billion per year

## Elder abuse

⇨ It is estimated that more than 500,000 older people in the UK are abused (roughly 5% of the older population)

⇨ Every hour, over 50 older people are neglected or abused in their own homes by family members, friends, neighbours or care workers

⇨ In a study based on 10,000 phone calls to a help-line up to 2004, the proportion of calls concerning the different types of elder abuse identified was as follows: psychological (34 per cent), financial (20 per cent), physical (19 per cent), sexual (3 per cent). 44 per cent of callers reported multiple abuse

## Long-term illness

⇨ 38% of people in Great Britain aged 65-74 and 50% of those aged 75+ have a limiting longstanding illness

⇨ Men in the UK can expect to live their last 6.7 years with a disability. For women, the average is 8.8 years

## Falls

⇨ Falls represent over half of hospital admissions for accidental injury

⇨ Half of those with hip fracture never regain their former level of function and one in five dies within three months

⇨ 50 to 70% of women will have an osteoporotic fracture at some time

## Sensory impairment

⇨ In the UK 42% of people over 75 will develop cataracts, almost 50% will have age-related macular degeneration

---

## 73% of older people in Great Britain agree that age discrimination exists in the daily lives of older people

---

⇨ 28% of people aged 65+ have difficulties with their eyesight

⇨ 55% of people aged 60+ are deaf or hard of hearing

## Mental health

⇨ Nearly 700,000 people are estimated to be suffering from dementia in the UK in 2007 and, by 2025, the number is expected to rise to one million

⇨ Alzheimer's affects 1 person in 4 over the age of 85. This rises to 1 in 3 for people over 90

⇨ Depression affects about 1 person in 8 over 65

## Incontinence

⇨ It is estimated that between 3 and 3.5 million people suffer from urinary incontinence in the UK. More than half are over 65 and the majority are women

## Strokes

⇨ There are over 100,000 first strokes every year in the UK, and 90% of these affect people over 65 years

## Arthritis

⇨ There are an estimated 9 million people in the UK suffering from arthritis

## Dying

⇨ Only 8.5 per cent of those dying of cancer aged over 85 die in a hospice, compared to 20 per cent of all cancer deaths

⇨ In the winter of 2006/7, there were an estimated 25,393 excess winter deaths of people aged 65 and over in the UK. About 93% of winter deaths are of people aged 65 and over

⇨ It has been estimated that for any degree colder than 20C, mortality rises by one to two per cent

⇨ Deaths from hypothermia are rare, but cold weather and poor heating can contribute to the deaths caused by circulatory diseases (responsible for 41% of all recorded deaths by natural causes) and by respiratory diseases (13%)

## National Health Service

⇨ Three-quarters of NHS clients are aged 65 and over but they receive only two-fifths of total expenditure

⇨ 9 per cent of people aged 75 and over in England find it very difficult to get to their doctor's surgery

⇨ Nearly one in five (19%) find it very difficult to get to their local hospital

## Care

⇨ In England, 346,700 people received home care services in 2007

⇨ Between 2000 and 2006, the number of households receiving home care services has decreased by over 13%

⇨ In 2007, there were estimated to be about 405,000 older people out of a total of 420,000 in residential care

⇨ The UK average annual fee for a single room in a private residential home is £23,504. For a nursing home, it is £33,280

## Older people as carers

⇨ There are between five and six million unpaid carers looking after a relative or friend

⇨ 2.8m people aged 50 and over provide unpaid care and 5% of people aged 85 provide unpaid care

⇨ Carers are currently saving the UK economy an estimated £87 billion per year

*July 2008*

⇨ The above information is reprinted with kind permission from Help the Aged. Visit www.helptheaged.org. uk for more information or to view sources for this article.

*© Help the Aged*

# Facts and figures: global ageing

## Information from HelpAge International

### The world is ageing

Ageing is a triumph of our times – a product of improved public health, sanitation and development. Yet over 100 million older people live on less than a dollar a day.*

⇨ In 1950, 8 out of every 100 people were over 60. By 2050, 22 out of every 100 people will be over 60.*

⇨ By 2045, the global population of people aged 60 years and over will likely surpass, for the first time in history, the number of children under age 15.*

⇨ The increasing share of older people in the world's population results from a combination of hugely increased life expectancy and reduced fertility. Total fertility is expected to decline from 2.82 children per woman in 1995-2000 to 2.15 children per woman in 2045-2050. Life expectancy worldwide is expected to increase by 11 years, from 65 in 1995-2000 to 76 in 2045-2050, despite the impact of HIV/AIDS.*

### Most of the world's older people live in developing countries

⇨ Even in the poorest countries, life expectancy is increasing and the number of older people is growing. In 2000, there were 374 million people over 60 in developing countries – 62% of the world's older people. In 2015, there will be 597 million older people in developing countries – 67% of the world's older people.*

⇨ In 2005, one in twelve people in developing countries is over 60. By 2015, one in ten people in developing countries will be over 60 and, by 2050, one in five people in developing countries will be over 60.*

⇨ In every region, the rate of population increase for the 65-and-over age group is higher than for the under-14 age group and the 15-64 age group.*

### There are more older women and they are more likely to be poor

⇨ The majority of older persons are women.*

⇨ In 2006, there are 82 men for every 100 women over 60 worldwide.*

⇨ In developing countries, the gap is less wide: there are 85 men for every 100 women over 60. However, with age this gap increases – for over-80s, there are only 73 men for every 100.*

⇨ Older women are more likely to be widowed, to live alone and in poverty. Source: Yvonne J. Gist and Victoria A. Velkoff, *Gender and Ageing: Demographic Dimensions*, International Programmes Centre, US Department of Commerce, 1997

⇨ Three of every four older poor individuals are women, with women being twice as likely to be living in poverty as men. Source: Choudhury, Sharmila and Michael V. Leonesio. 1997. Life-Cycle Aspects of Poverty among Older Women, *Social Security Bulletin*, 60(2): 17-36

### Older people care for people with HIV/AIDS and orphans

⇨ Older people are the primary carers for orphaned and vulnerable children affected by HIV/AIDS and those living with HIV/AIDS. Source: *Building blocks: Africa-wide briefing notes – supporting older carers*, HIV AIDS Alliance and HelpAge International, 2004

⇨ In Botswana, Namibia, Malawi, South Africa, Tanzania and Zimbabwe, up to 60 per cent of orphaned children live in grandparent-headed households. Source: Monasch,R and JT Boerma 2004 cited in *AIDS: the frontline: Supporting older carers of people living with HIV/AIDS and orphaned children in Mozambique, South Africa and Sudan*, the Global Coalition on Women and AIDS, December 2005

In Botswana, Namibia, Malawi, South Africa, Tanzania and Zimbabwe, up to 60 per cent of orphaned children live in grandparent-headed households

⇨ In Thailand, older people care for two-thirds of younger adults who die of AIDS and almost half of all orphans live with their grandparents. Source: Knodel, J et al, AIDS and older persons: the view from Thailand, *PSC Research Report*, 2-497, February 2002

*Source: UNDESA, *Population Ageing Wallchart 2006 (800kb pdf)*, Population Division 2006
Modified 2 July 2007

⇨ The above information is reprinted with kind permission from HelpAge International. Visit www.helpage.org for more information.
© HelpAge International

# 10 facts on ageing and the life course

## Information from the World Health Organisation

Long life is a sign of good health. The ageing of the world's population – in developing and developed countries – is an indicator of improving global health. The world's elderly population – people 60 years of age and older – is 650 million. By 2050, the 'greying' population is forecast to reach 2 billion.

Along with this positive trend, however, come special health challenges for the 21st century. Preparing health providers and societies to meet the needs of elderly people is essential: training for health professionals on old-age care; preventing and managing age-associated chronic diseases; designing sustainable policies on long-term care; and developing age-friendly services and settings.

### Fact 1

Ageing is a global phenomenon. The world's elderly population – people 60 years of age and older – is the fastest growing age group. By 2050 about 80% of the elderly will be living in developing countries. Population ageing is occurring in parallel with rapid urbanisation: in 2007 more than half of the world's population live in cities. By 2030 that figure is expected to rise to more than 60%.

### Fact 2

Population ageing is a triumph of modern society. It reflects improving global health, but also raises special challenges for the 21st century in both developing and developed countries. In 2005, life expectancy in countries like Japan and France was already more than 80 years. Life expectancy is also rising in developing countries: a child born today in Chile, Costa Rica, Jamaica, Lebanon, Sri Lanka or Thailand can expect to live for more than 70 years.

### Fact 3

Vast health inequalities persist, as is clear from differences in life expectancy at birth. For example, while Japan has the highest life expectancy in the world at 82.2 years, in several countries in Africa the figure is as much as 40 years lower.

### Fact 4

Within countries, health inequalities are also significant. For example, in the United States of America higher socioeconomic groups can expect to live up to 20 years longer than those from lower socioeconomic groups.

### Fact 5

By 2050, close to 80% of all deaths are expected to occur in people older than 60. Health expenditure increases with age and is concentrated in the last year of life – but the older a person dies, the less costs are concentrated in that period. Postponing the age of death through healthy ageing combined with appropriate end-of-life policies could lead to major health care savings.

### Fact 6

Healthy older people also represent a resource for their families, communities and economies. Investing in health throughout life produces dividends for societies everywhere. It is rarely too late to change risky behaviours to promote health: for example, the risk of premature death decreases by 50% if someone gives up smoking between 60 and 75 years of age.

### Fact 7

Effective, community-level primary health care for older people is crucial to promote health, prevent disease and manage chronic illnesses in dependent and frail patients. In general, training for health professionals includes little if any instruction about care for the elderly. However, they will increasingly spend time caring for this section of the population. WHO maintains that all health providers should be trained on ageing issues, regardless of their specialism.

### Fact 8

Disasters and emergencies severely impact the most vulnerable, including older people. As examples: the highest percentage of fatalities in Indonesia caused by the 2004 Indian Ocean tsunami was in people 60 years of age and older, and the majority of the 2003 heatwave victims in Europe were people 70 years of age and older. Policies to protect older persons during emergencies are urgently required.

### Fact 9

In older age, the risk of falls increases and consequences of injuries are far more serious. This leads to significant health, human and economic costs. In Australia, the average health system cost per one fall-related injury for people 65 years of age and older was US$ 3611 in 2001-2002.

### Fact 10

Elder abuse is on the increase as the population ages and social dynamics change. WHO estimates that between 4% and 6% of older persons worldwide have suffered from a form of elder abuse – either physical, psychological, emotional, financial or due to neglect. Elder abuse is an infringement of human rights.

*28 September 2007*

⇨ The above information is reprinted with kind permission from the World Health Organisation. Visit www.who.int for more information.

# Profile of the UK's older people

## Information from Ipsos MORI

To celebrate International Older People's Day Ipsos MORI has released a new analysis of our data on older people. Ipsos MORI's data points to a diverse group whose contribution to society and potential productivity is often overlooked by Government and society.

Official figures show that people aged 65 and over currently account for a sixth of the UK population, but the baby-boom generation are sweeping into their 60s and set to boost the population of pensioners to a quarter by 2031. The profile of the older population is rapidly changing as baby boomers age, and older people increasingly have more diverse views and behaviours than previous generations, reflecting wider changes in society.

### 'Sure and steady' Brown gaining among the Grey Gordons – should Cameron be worried?

➪ Ipsos MORI's data shows that most older people are politically literate and socially engaged. The older age groups are far more likely to vote than younger people, indeed a quarter of the voters at the 2005 general election were aged 65+, and more than two in five were aged 55 or over.

➪ Furthermore, older voters are less volatile in their party support than the young and middle-aged, probably because their party loyalties are more deeply ingrained. This may mean that they are harder for the parties to win over, but also implies that once convinced they are more likely to stay convinced.

➪ Older people remain a bedrock of Conservative support and they are less satisfied with the Government than younger people (although since Brown took over as Labour leader, support for Labour among this group has increased by 5 percentage points in July and August).

➪ However, David Cameron will be worried about his personal ratings among older people. They are the most dissatisfied age group with his performance and, looking at the aggregate data for the first two months of Brown's premiership, his scores are falling faster among older people than voters as a whole. Furthermore, Brown's 'sure and steady' persona seems to be playing well among older people. Although his overall ratings are still higher among the under-55s, Brown's satisfaction score among older people is much higher than Tony Blair's in the last months of his premiership.

---

## Most older people are politically literate and socially engaged

---

### A new age of opportunity?

Older people have more to contribute to society than ever before – they will live longer than previous generations, they are healthier and are growing in numbers and influence. The contribution of older people to society in terms of volunteering, citizenship and consumer spending is disproportionately high. Yet the time, skills and resources that older people have to offer society often appear to be undervalued and untapped. We argue that as the ageing population increases, so does the window of opportunity for them to become more active.

Jo Slaymaker of Ipsos MORI said: 'As a society we need to radically change our ideas about what old age means. The old stereotypes are now simply outdated, and the politicians and companies that understand this best will benefit.'

Older people are more satisfied with their standard of living than their younger counterparts (over 80% of 65+s, compared with 71% of the middle-aged). Furthermore, many people reaching 'old age' are empty-nesters and have more time to relax and have fun than their younger relatives. They have plenty of leisure time and more disposable income than ever before.

Contrary to the stereotype of 'old age', retirees are likely to be active,

with many enjoying overseas holidays (43% of 65-74s) and voluntary work (30% of 65-74s). Three-quarters of 65- to 74-year-olds have paid off their mortgage and can rely on significant capital in homes. The 55- to 64-year-old age group are also about as happy with their sex lives as younger people, so old age isn't all doom and gloom.

---

## Participation in leisure activities is high for 50- to 69-year-olds but activity falls steeply after 70

---

Participation in leisure activities is high for 50- to 69-year-olds but activity falls steeply after 70. But inactivity is not just about poor health. The main reason that older people say they don't go out more is fear of crime (25% of 65-74s and 20% of 75+s). Public transport is also vital (only half of 75+s

have access to a car) and even the little things help – those aged over 70 are three times as likely to say that road and pavement repairs are important in making somewhere a good place to live than those aged under 45.

*Old age is not a bed of roses for everyone*

Yet for many, 'old age' represents a period of low productivity, frailty, bad health and decline. In particular, health notably deteriorates in later life – particularly for those aged 75+ (three-fifths report having a limiting long-standing illness or disability) – and many face barriers to leading a social, healthy and active life in later years. 'Active ageing', and social participation can protect older people against loneliness and isolation. It's interesting that whilst younger people think that being financially comfortable is key to having a happy old age, for older people, social interaction and independence are just as important. Up to a quarter of over-75s say they have gone a full day

without anyone speaking to them.

Thoughtful communication about the kinds of activities and opportunities available for older people to get involved in, and importantly how to access them, is key to social inclusion and active ageing. This will become increasingly vital for central and local Government to address as the population ages. A shrewd Government and society will ensure that what is currently a somewhat untapped resource is used more wisely and valued more highly. This means maximising accessibility to services, leisure activities, public transport and volunteering; providing joined-up services that focus on people's mental and physical well-being; and maximising opportunity for participation and inclusion.
*30 September 2007*

⇨ The above information is re-printed with kind permission from Ipsos MORI. Visit www.ipsos-mori.com for more information.
© *Ipsos MORI*

# Age discrimination

## Information from the Equality and Human Rights Commission

Unlawful age discrimination happens when someone is treated unfavourably because of their age, without justification, or is harassed or victimised because of their age.

### Does age discrimination apply to me?

Age discrimination law currently applies only in employment and vocational training where you have been treated less favourably on the basis of your age, without justification. This may be because you are considered too young or too old.

Age discrimination law does not currently apply to goods and services, though human rights law may give some protection in these areas.

Legally, the test for many potential cases of age discrimination is whether the discrimination can be said to be 'justified'. Unlike most other types of

discrimination, justification can be used lawfully as a defence for direct age discrimination, as well as indirect age discrimination.

### What is age discrimination?
For definitions of the different types of discrimination, such as direct, indirect, harassment and victimisation.

The following are examples of age discrimination:
⇨ An employer refuses to offer a job to a young candidate, even though the candidate has the skills and competencies required for it. The employer sees the position as one of authority and does not feel the young candidate will be respected or taken seriously because of his age. This is an example of direct discrimination.
⇨ An employer insists that all candidates for a job have to meet a physical fitness test (that

younger candidates can meet more easily) even though the fitness standard is not required for the job in question. This is indirect discrimination.
⇨ An employee has been consistently passed over for promotion, and is not allowed to attend meetings unaccompanied, because she looks young for her age. Her manager, who is 10 years older than her, feels that she is too 'wet behind the ears' to be given more responsibility, despite the fact that she has the right qualifications and five years' experience in her role. This is an example of direct discrimination.
⇨ A general work culture appears to tolerate people telling ageist jokes, bullying or name calling. This could count as harassment on the grounds of age. Harassment is a form of direct discrimination.
⇨ As one of its requirements, a job

advert lists 10 years' experience in a relevant field, when two or three years' experience would be adequate for the job. This could be seen as indirect discrimination.

## When and where could age discrimination take place?

People can encounter unlawful age discrimination at work and in education and training.

---

**Age discrimination law currently applies only in employment and vocational training where you have been treated less favourably on the basis of your age, without justification**

---

*Working and earning*

An example of direct age discrimination in employment would be an IT company with a policy of not recruiting older employees because they didn't fit in with the youthful culture of the company. Age discrimination legislation applies throughout employment: from recruitment advertising to pension rules. However, there are circumstances in which age discrimination is allowed. See the section below on 'When is age discrimination lawful?'.

*Vocational learning and training*

The opportunity to learn and receive training should be open to all, and educational providers at institutions of further and higher education are covered by age regulations. An example would be a 16-year-old who applies for a vocational training course to enhance her promotion opportunities within her company. She is refused entry to the company's training scheme on the grounds that she is too young. Under age regulations her employer would not be allowed to prevent her from seeking further training because of her age.

However, it can sometimes be justifiable to adopt an age-specific approach to the delivery of vocational education or training – provided this

is a fair means of achieving a genuine aim. An example of this would be an educational institution that increases the participation of a particular age group on a training course to ensure that this section of the population is integrated into the workforce. This is an example of positive action, which is discussed further below.

### When is age discrimination lawful?

In certain circumstances, age discrimination may be lawful, but there must be an 'objective justification' in every case.

*Objective justification*

An objective justification allows an employer to discriminate both directly and indirectly on the basis of age. They must, however, show that this discrimination is 'proportionate' and contributes to a 'legitimate' aim.

Proportionate means that:

⇨ what the employer is doing is actually achieving its aim;

⇨ the discriminatory effect should be significantly outweighed by the importance and benefits of the legitimate aim;

⇨ the employer should have no reasonable alternative to the action they are taking. If the legitimate aim can be achieved by another or less discriminatory means, they must then opt for that route. Legitimate means:

↳ economic factors such as the needs of and the efficiency of running a business;

↳ the health, welfare and safety of the individual (including protection of young people or older workers);

↳ the particular training requirements of the job.

A legitimate aim must correspond with a legitimate need of the employer. For example, economic efficiency may be a real aim but saving money because discrimination is cheaper than non-discrimination is not a legitimate need. It is not easy to prove objective justification, and employers have to provide valid evidence if they are challenged.

For example, some employers have policies that link pay and benefits to an employee's length of service, such as additional holiday entitlement for long-serving employees. This may indirectly discriminate against younger people who are less likely to have been employed for that length of time, but in most circumstances it is seen as being a proportionate way of encouraging staff loyalty.

*A genuine occupational requirement*

In some circumstances, it may be lawful for an employer to treat people differently if there is a 'genuine occupational requirement' for a job holder to be of a particular age. For example, a younger actress would be required to play the role of a female teenager in a film.

*Positive action*

The term 'positive action' refers to legal measures that are designed to counteract the effects of past discrimination and to help abolish stereotyping. Positive action can be taken to encourage people from particular age groups to take advantage of opportunities for training or work experience schemes, or encourage them to apply for

particular employment. It can only be done when a particular group has been identified as under-represented in a certain area of employment. Positive action may include things like introducing fair selection procedures, training programmes or targeting job advertisements at a particular group.

Positive action is not the same as positive discrimination, and does not involve treating particular groups more favourably when recruiting. Employers must make sure that employees are hired or promoted on merit alone.

For example, a company with a young workforce which does not typically attract applications from older people could advertise a job vacancy by saying: 'We would welcome applications from candidates over the age of 45, as this age group is currently under-represented within our establishment. However, the appointment will be made on merit alone.'

There are a few other exemptions:

⇨ the national minimum wage is split into three different rates depending on the age of the employee. Therefore it is within the law for employers to pay their employees minimum wages of different rates according to their age.

⇨ employment can depend on age if this is required by existing law. For example, the position of a bar tender serving alcohol at a club can only be filled by someone who is over 18 years of age, to comply with licensing requirements.

⇨ volunteers generally don't have protection from discrimination, unless their unpaid work is part of a training course or they are government-appointed office holders (like magistrates, for example).

⇨ age discrimination legislation does not cover the provision of goods and services, which means that it is lawful for insurance companies and healthcare providers, for example, to discriminate on the grounds of age.

### What does the law say?

Legislation relating to age discrim-ination includes the following:

*The Employment Equality (Age) Regulations 2006: Legislation effective from October 2006 means that employers can no longer discriminate against employees on grounds of age.*

⇨ The above information is reprinted with kind permission from the Equality and Human Rights Commission. Visit www.equalityhumanrights.com for more information.

*© Equality and Human Rights Commission*

# Number of working pensioners continues to rise

### Information from The Age and Employment Network

Commenting on today's employment figures, Chris Ball, Chief Executive of TAEN –The Age and Employment Network, said:

'Today's news that the number of working pensioners is continuing to rise* – up by 30,000 – is significant. While it is encouraging to know that there are increasing opportunities for some people to go on working, there are many more who would like to work and the number is rising all the time as the inflation rate for pensioners rises above that for other members of society.

'We estimate that perhaps double the present number working want, or need, paid work – not just to pay for life's "little luxuries" but for the basics of food, fuel and lighting.

'Unfortunately, the rising figures mask the fact that many employers have decided that once their employees reach 65, they are deemed to be past their "use-by date". This is an absurd waste of fit and able people who have scarce knowledge and skills. It damages organisations and the economy.

'Employers are being aided and abetted in this unfair and absurd discrimination against older workers by the Age Discrimination Regulations which make it lawful to fire people merely because they have reached that age.

'We are once again calling on the Government to bring forward its review of the Default Retirement Age** so that not only those individuals, their families and communities, but also the wider economy can benefit from their active involvement and contribution to the British labour market.'

### Notes

* According to today's employment figures from the Office for National Statistics, the number of people working over state pension age (60 for women and 65 for men) increased in the 3 months from September to November 2007 by 35,000 to 1.268 million. All the increase was amongst women over state pension age.

** The Default Retirement Age: under the Equal Employment (Age) Regulations 2006 it is lawful for an employer to dismiss an employee once they reach the age of 65 or later, providing they follow the correct procedure. Under that procedure an employee can request to work on but the employer can refuse the request (and a subsequent appeal) without giving reasons for the refusal.

The Default Retirement Age is the subject of the 'Heyday' challenge currently before the European Court of Justice and the President of the Employment Tribunal Service for England has put a 'stay' on all tribunal cases involving the Default Retirement Age for the time being.

*17 January 2008*

⇨ The above information is reprinted with kind permission from The Age and Employment Network. Visit www.taen.org.uk for more information.

*© TAEN*

# Knowledge of age laws increasing

## Increased awareness of age laws spells trouble for employers

⇨ *86% of Brits know it's illegal to discriminate on age at work.*

⇨ *But 16 million workers have witnessed ageist practices at work in the last year alone.*

⇨ *Leading think tank on age issues calls for more change on the ground as employer/employee expectations just don't match.*

On 1st October 2006 age discrimination became unlawful. Twelve months later, awareness of the legislation has almost doubled to become widespread – yet new research commissioned by the Employers Forum on Age (EFA) has found that employers are still not abiding by the rules.

The EFA research reveals that almost nine out of ten (86%) people know it is illegal to discriminate on the grounds of age at work, compared to just 51% this time last year. Shockingly the survey also found that ageism is still endemic in the workplace, with 16 million (59%) workers claiming to have witnessed ageist behaviour in the workplace during the last twelve months alone, compared to 61% when surveyed just before the legislation came in.

Sam Mercer, Chief Executive of the Employers Forum on Age, commented: 'It is great that awareness of age discrimination issues among British adults has increased at an impressive pace since the law was passed twelve months ago. This proves that the laws served a purpose in terms of getting ageism on the radar. However, it is bad news for those employers who are still falling well short of the required standards of practice. On average 200 age discrimination claims are lodged every month with the Employment Tribunal Service, no employer can afford to bury their head in the sand and hope this issue will just go away.'

⇨ Nearly one-third (30%) of workers are aware of an older person getting paid more than a younger person for doing the same job.

⇨ One in three (31%) see people being managed differently depending on their age – an increase from 23% last year.

---

**Almost nine out of ten (86%) people know it is illegal to discriminate on the grounds of age at work**

---

⇨ Over one in eight (15%) have had a younger person in the workplace overlooked for promotion in favour of an older person, irrespective of experience – this is down from last year which was 23%.

⇨ More than a quarter (27%) said that people of a similar age to the rest of the team are recruited to ensure a good 'fit'. This has not changed in the 12 months since the laws came into force.

The EFA research also found that there is a long way to go in ensuring that ageism is properly understood, with less than half (45%) of those surveyed correctly identifying that it is an issue which can affect anyone of any age and a third (33%) believing that it only affects older people.

Mercer continues: 'While it is encouraging that awareness of the law is high, it is vital that we wake up to the fact that ageism affects people of all ages and is not just an issue for older people. One area where older people are specifically affected, however, is retirement. A staggering 92% of people surveyed think they should have the right to work for as long as they like if they are able to do the job, regardless of their age. However, one in five (21%) said that their employer would not give them this right, and instead would use the default retirement age of 65. This disparity between employees' expectations and the flexibility employers are prepared to offer will inevitably lead to tension. It is time for employers to think seriously about following in the footsteps of some leading EFA members and removing mandatory retirement ages.'

Mercer concludes, 'Age discrimination laws have been in effect for one year, and good progress has been made in some areas. However, ageist attitudes are still ingrained and changing that culture is a much bigger task, but one which cannot be avoided.'
*28 September 2007*

⇨ The above information is reprinted with kind permission from the Employers Forum on Age. Visit www. efa.org.uk for more information.
© *Employers Forum on Age*

# Work experienced

## Information from Birmingham Midshires

In the week when Nick Ross left the BBC, allegedly due to his age, new research reveals that, in fact, older people are more valued in the workplace than their younger colleagues. Birmingham Midshires' 'Life 2' campaign, which explores the issues affecting the lifestyle of the over-55s, reveals that just three per cent of people in this age group have suffered age discrimination at work, compared to 11 per cent of young people[1].

One in two (50%) under-25-year-olds who said they had been discriminated against claim that they were not given a job due to their age and 48 per cent were actually told that their prospective employers were looking for someone older. In contrast, just 35 per cent of over-55s were told a company wanted to recruit someone younger. With the average age of a FTSE 100 chief executive standing at 52[2], it appears that people in their fifth decade really are in the golden age of their careers.

The most common form of discrimination cited by those unhappy with their treatment was being overlooked for a promotion (52%) or sidelined on work or projects (34%). Almost one in four (23%) of those suffering age discrimination feel socially excluded at work and one in five (19%) have been the victims of name calling.

As Nick Ross and Moira Stewart may be able to testify[3], the media is the most unforgiving career-choice, with 43% of those working in the field feeling uncomfortable in their current job, or experiencing difficulties when trying to gain new employment. Meanwhile, bosses in the retail sector are least likely to allow an employee's age to cloud their judgement.

---

**One in two (50%) under-25-year-olds who said they had been discriminated against claim that they were not given a job due to their age**

---

Public sector workers are also more circumspect when it comes to respecting colleagues regardless of their age, with 74 per cent of people reporting no problems. However, people working in the travel and leisure industry may struggle, with 37 per cent experiencing some form of ageism.

More men than women have reported difficulties (32 per cent of men, compared to 27 per cent of women) but while men may be the butt of office banter and feel excluded socially, women are more likely to suffer serious consequences such as being overlooked for promotion or sidelined on projects.

Conforming to the 'city boy' stereotype, Londoners are most likely to experience ageism (33%) while Scotland is the home of meritocracy (27% falling victim to age-related problems). People in Wales are most likely to be called names (23%), but those in the South are at most risk of being laid off due to their years (18%).

Jason Robinson, director of savings operations for Birmingham Midshires, said: 'While discrimination against any age group is unacceptable, there has long been a view that older people are likely to be overtaken by younger colleagues several years before they are ready to retire. This research shows a heartening appetite for experience – with those in their 40s and 50s embracing change at work and remaining top of their game.'

1. 'Young people' refers to those aged 18 to 24 years.
2. The Egremont research, as reported in *The Sunday Times*, 18 February 2007.
3. Moira Stewart was axed by the BBC in March, allegedly due to her age.

*21 June 2007*

⇨ The above information is reprinted with kind permission from Birmingham Midshires. Visit www.askbm.co.uk for more information.

© *Birmingham Midshires*

SORRY, TOO YOUNG

SORRY, TOO OLD

SORRY, NOT ENOUGH EXPERIENCE

SORRY, OVERQUALIFIED

# Plans to outlaw age discrimination announced

## Information from politics.co.uk

The government has announced plans today to reduce age discrimination within the UK workforce.

Equalities minister Harriet Harman presented the proposals to MPs on Thursday as part of the equalities bill.

The plans, to be introduced across England, Wales and Scotland, will also aim to tackle gender pay differences.

Campaigners have long claimed age discrimination is widespread in today's society. They point in particular at the NHS where older patients may be told to expect poor health at their age or denied treatment outright.

Ms Harman defended the bill, which some have claimed discriminates against white men, on GMTV this morning.

'Most women are going out to work and they are just as committed to their jobs – the money that they earn is important to the household budget so they should be paid fairly,' she said.

'Yet listen to this figure – if you are a woman working part-time you get 40 per cent less per hour on average than a man working full-time.

'Now either this is because women are not up to the job or else there is discrimination against them. You can't challenge discrimination when it's kept swept under the carpet. I think there's a lot of resentment at the unfairness against women. They are not being given the facts.'

In the Commons, later this morning, Ms Harman declared that 'fairness' was important for British society and economy.

She also called for employers to be forced into publishing data on key equality issues.

Ms Harman said that the private sector was particularly guilty of inequality when it came to pay.

Eighty per cent of British workers are employed in the private sector, which Ms Harman claims has a pay gap twice as big as the public sector.

She also claimed that the government would be aiming to overturn current discrimination against the elderly.

'Many people still think it's perfectly acceptable to discriminate against the elderly, it is not,' she said, adding: 'People are not over the hill at 60.'

'We will promote equality for older people.'

The equalities minister also announced that it should be possible to see which businesses were employing disabled people and which were 'shutting them out'.

In response, Age Concern and Help the Aged claimed the government's plans were a 'massive step forward'.

Michael Lake, director general of Help the Aged, said: 'For a long time the government would not accept that age discrimination was a problem. Now it has, and so the timetable for action is absolutely crucial.

'Older people have been waiting for far too long to be treated as equals – and they shouldn't have to wait for these rights any longer. Legislation must be enacted without delay so older people can be on a truly equal footing as soon as possible.'

Age Concern's director general, Gordon Lishman, added: 'The government's decision to use the equality bill to outlaw age discrimination is fantastic news. It sends a clear signal that ageism should be taken as seriously as any other form of discrimination. This legislation will transform the lives of millions of older people by giving them the same opportunities to participate in society as everyone else.'

But proposals on workplace equality have been widely derided. Even

Progressive Vision, a classic liberal think tank, called the plans 'ludicrous' and 'a recipe for disaster'.

Mark Littlewood, Progressive Vision's communications director, said: 'To allow gender or race to act as a tie-breaker in a close contest is offensive and immoral.

'If being a white man can be the determining factor in failing to get a job, where will this logically end?

'These proposals will lead to resentment, arbitrary decision-taking and risk making discrimination in Britain worse not better.'

The NHS may tell older patients to expect poor health at their age or deny them treatment outright

Liberal Democrats said the plans did not tackle inequality in the private sector.

'Efforts to tackle entrenched inequality are welcome, but serious questions must be asked about why the private sector is getting off so lightly,' said Lib Dem equality spokesperson Lynne Featherstone.

'A voluntary audit system for private industry is hardly worth the paper it's printed on. We need to know when the government actually plans to step in if progress isn't made.'
26 June 2008

⇨ The above information is reprinted with kind permission from politics.co.uk. Visit www.politics.co.uk for more information.
© politics.co.uk

# Ignoring old age won't keep you young

**By Andrew O'Hagan**

The greatest contradiction in modern life is also one that nobody ever mentions – that today's youth is obsessed with living for ever, but has no respect for the elderly.

How can a generation yearn to escape every illness and defy the clock while, at the same time, give no thought to what life is like for old people?

We might call it a contradiction and we might call it bad preparation; we also might call it plain stupid, and soon enough Britain will have a population of the super-elderly living on in a place rigged up to meet the interests of 25-year-olds.

One of our greatest challenges will be to increase our capacity to deal with the needs of an ageing population, and, on current trends, we are already failing at it.

According to a report published yesterday by the independent think tank Reform, the NHS is likely to decline as the current population grows old, leaving those who gave little thought to the realities of agedness in a whole lot of trouble.

What we have is a generation of Gonerils and Regans, snapping youths who imagine the elderly to have failed some crucial test of coolness, as if youth were itself a very superior kind of knowledge.

Well, it is not. It is a rather familiar kind of ignorance, and one that is reluctant to make concessions to the value of experience.

Growing old is now considered more of an option than an inevitability, something to beat rather than be resigned to, something that is thought to take away from one's individuality rather than deepen it.

Of all the vanities of the current period, this might be the gravest. Apart from being unkind to our seniors, it leaves us with half a life, half a view of what it might mean to be alive. I'll be 40 this year and

I already feel suffocated by youth culture, so what on earth must it be like for people twice my age?

News came this week of a 101-year-old gentleman who is about to be kicked out of New Zealand by the immigration authorities. The latter are worried that the man could become a drain on health resources.

## The greatest contradiction in modern life is also one that nobody ever mentions – that today's youth is obsessed with living for ever, but has no respect for the elderly

The figures speak for themselves: more than 100,000 Britons were granted residency permits for New Zealand last year, and most of them were young. The 101-year-old man has only one relative, his son, who lives in New Zealand; yet the authorities consider it too much to ask that the old boy gets to live out his last years in comfort.

What a disastrous, callous decision. The man has savings and a pension, but somehow it is understood that he would be a better bet for citizenship if he were a callow 22-year-old who wanted to drink his way around the North Island.

We are now routinely advised by medical experts on how to make it to 90. The cult of longevity has become everything: the point is to live long, not live well; the point is to stick around in the world, not to improve it.

Like King Lear, we might find in future that to be four-score-and-ten is less fun than it looked from the vantage point of the self-loving thirtysomething.

Old people are Britain's biggest minority and it seems shocking that their voice is so dimmed: they have paid more into the country than any other group, yet the country does not appear to serve them or consider them quite so much.

As a society, we make respectful noises about our elderly, but in daily life we want to drown them out or ignore them. It can be only a matter of energy that stops the British elderly from being the angriest and most vocal minority in Europe.

Meanwhile, the national indulgence of immaturity has led us into another new corner: according to the organisation that represents funeral directors, people no longer show respect to funeral cortèges and ignore burial customs.

I saw this trend in all its glory the other week, when I attended a funeral in the north. Impatient drivers tried to cut up the driver of the hearse; at one point, someone actually tooted a horn at a roundabout as the funeral cars went round at a slow pace.

And in the town, I was struck that no one took off his hat. There they all were, the laughing boys and girls in their baseball caps, and the black cars went past and they didn't see them.

The hospitals aren't ready for these people to get old, but, much more, the people themselves aren't ready. They are surrounded by a culture that wants to tell them how to live to 90, but nobody has any sense of what that will actually mean on the ground.

They think it means they will be 25 for ever and ever. But whose fault is this? Drivers who don't give way to funeral cortèges are not the fault of governments or legislators. They are casualties of their own dullness, people who lack the imagination to think beyond the confines of their own life, and that is a very impoverished place to be.

Empathy with old people is not just a do-gooder's philosophy – it is a form of self-interest. With any luck, we will all have our turn at shuffling down the high street. A culture that does not know how to look after its elderly is a brutal one, a vicious one, and ultimately a self-defeating one.

We may find one day that we failed to honour the single greatest certainty in our lives: that we, too, would grow old and die. My generation might turn out to be the first one to be truly shocked by this certainty. And history might conclude that a people who never knew how to grow old never really knew how to live.

*12 February 2008*

© *Telegraph Group Limited, London 2008*

# Reinventing the retirement cliff edge

## Information from the Department for Work and Pensions

Less than half of Britons chose the word 'happy' to describe how they felt on the first day of retirement, evidence the traditional sudden stop approach no longer works for many people.

New research by Ipsos MORI shows a mixed bag of emotions for those waking up on day one of retirement with under a third saying they felt relaxed and under a quarter feeling free. A surprising one in ten felt anxious, sad or lost.

---

### Less than half of Britons chose the word 'happy' to describe how they felt on the first day of retirement

---

Pensions Minister Mike O'Brien comments:

'The idea that one day you work and the next you stop can be a shock to the system. These findings challenge the traditional "one size fits all" approach to retirement. Many of today's older workers are rejecting the cliff edge between work and retirement in favour of a gradual step down. And employers should help them to do this.'

Over 1000 people over 55 were interviewed to find out their views on retirement and work. People approaching retirement admitted there's lots they'll miss about their jobs when they stop. Topping their miss list are work friends, being challenged, office banter and a reason to get out of the house.

Soon to be retirees are equally candid about what they'll be happy to turn their backs on. While their distaste for the work canteen, office politics and commuting is unlikely to raise eyebrows, it may come as a surprise that three-quarters of Brits are looking forward to binning the Christmas party. Oddly, one in ten people confesses they'll miss the journey to and from work.

When asked why they still work, extra cash was a top motivator followed closely by over half doing it because they enjoy their jobs. A third cited keeping the mind active or keeping fit and over a quarter said they'd miss work if they stopped. Interestingly, the number of people who felt too young to stop increased with age from just under a third of 55- to 64-year-olds to nearly half of those 65- to 74-year-olds surveyed.

The stepping-down approach is reaping dividends with part-time workers enjoying greater job satisfaction than their full-time counterparts – nearly half said they would miss work if they stopped compared to just over a quarter of full-timers. Over one million Brits are already working past state pension age and most of these have chosen to work part-time. With people living longer, healthier lives this trend looks set to continue.

This month marks the start of a two-year countdown to state pension age changes for women, which sees the state pension age for women start to gradually rise from 60 to 65 from 6th April 2010.

Mike O'Brien adds:

'Women's state pension age is moving but you don't have to retire at this date. You have time to plan and you may be surprised by the choices you have. You could use your state pension to allow you to work part-time or choose to put off taking it and get extra pension later or a lump sum. To get the facts, put your birthday into the Pension Service website and it'll tell you when you can get your state pension.'

*8 April 2008*

⇨ The above information is reprinted with kind permission from the Department for Work and Pensions. Visit www.dwp.gov.uk for more information.

© *Crown copyright*

# Dignified conclusions

**A three-year, government-backed study will examine the risk of abuse and neglect of older people in care homes and on NHS wards. But how prevalent is the problem, and how can we tackle it? We ask the experts**

### Katie Ghose
### Director, British Institute of Human Rights

Finally, we have a cast-iron guarantee that the Human Rights Act loophole for care homes will be closed right away. Older and disabled care home residents can now expect legal change in a matter of weeks. This is hugely important, not only because the vast majority of residents who live in private and voluntary-run care homes will be able to use the act to challenge abuses such as malnutrition, over-sedation, and unfair home closures, but also because of the incentive this will create for care home managers and staff to ensure that human rights are respected in the first place. BIHR knows from its work that there is an important relationship between enforceable legal remedies and the creation of a wider human rights' culture that would see all care providers actively embracing human rights as a driver towards providing the very best and tailored care to all human beings who walk through their door.

### Daniel Blake
### Policy manager, Action on Elder Abuse

A good care home is not necessarily a care home that has no abuse. A good care home is one that responds appropriately, robustly and quickly to allegations of abuse. Because of the nature of this sector – providing mass accommodation for a large number of people – it would be surprising if there was no abuse. It's very difficult to get a handle on its extent – it can be difficult for people to know where to report concerns. Only 5% of elderly people live in care homes, but 20% of calls to our helpline are about abuse in care homes, and the proportionality of that is worrying. However, most elderly people are abused in their own home by family. There is a very negative public perception of care homes. To change that perception we need more research and understanding. [The minister for social care] Ivan Lewis put it very well – if it's not acceptable for my mum then it's not acceptable for anyone – and that should be the benchmark. We need to put dignity at the heart of the issue.

### Bridget Penhale
### Reader in gerontology, Sheffield University

We don't know enough about the prevalence of abuse and neglect in care homes and hospital settings. Some of the most vulnerable older people live in care homes, often with complex conditions and/or multiple disabilities, and individuals or their relatives may be afraid to speak out about what is happening for fear of making a situation worse. It is also possible that people do not know quite what care to expect from care homes and will accept explanations for certain treatment as 'coming from those who know'. Many, perhaps even the majority, of care homes provide appropriate and high quality care that meets the needs of the residents. Homes that are proactive in protecting residents, that have well-developed complaints procedures and processes concerning abuse and neglect, may well have less problems, as their message is: 'If we come across a problem we will deal with it,' rather than: 'This could never happen here.' We know that the difference between a good, well-functioning home and a poor quality, abusive home is not very great, and situations can change very quickly. We need to be vigilant and we need sound and robust inspection processes. We need to promote positive images of residential care, and invest in care homes and their staff. Staff are often part-time, very poorly paid and with few opportunities for training and development. If staff are not valued highly enough for the work they do, should we be surprised if this leads to mistreatment of the residents they are supposed to care for?

### Roger Clough
### Emeritus professor of social care, Lancaster University

Abuse is a term that's often used very loosely. It is very important to distinguish between good practice, poor practice and unacceptably bad practice. We need to understand what it is that produces poor practice – quality of leadership, or not employing staff with enough qualifications, and that includes pay. If we understand [this] then we can eliminate it. I feel very strongly that there's a stereotypical image of residential homes as places where everyone sits around waiting to die. Some places are offering the best possible option for those who can't find care elsewhere. We have to recognise as a society that for some older people a residential care home is the very best place you can live. People have to think of it as their main option if they are unable to live in their own homes. A residential home has got to be seen as part of the community and as a community in its own right.

### Stephen Burke
### Chief executive, Counsel and Care

Care homes aren't islands. They are part of their local community. By being more open and transparent this would enable the public to see the quality of care that is given. A quarter of inquiries to our advice line are about issues around care homes and quality of care; 22% of homes don't deliver to minimum standards. We must ensure that people have access to independent advocacy in order to make complaints. Some are too frail or don't have family to help. Media coverage suggests there are very real concerns. There is a negative public perception – but a lot of this stems from negative media coverage as well as bad practice in care homes. There are a lot of good care homes. We need to recognise that many elderly people coming into care homes now will have dementia – and we need to meet these needs. We would like to see the human rights legislation extended to people in all care homes. And we need to tackle issues of underfunding – there is a huge squeeze on resources – which is bound to have a negative impact on care.

### Kate Jopling
*Head of public affairs, Help the Aged*

It is very difficult to say how wide-spread the problem [of indignity and abuse] is. We hear about a tiny number of cases which are probably the tip of the iceberg. Elderly people often have nowhere to go to complain – and it's only when family members get involved that it becomes known. We estimate that there are about 5,000 cases of elder abuse happening at any one time. There are lots of excellent care homes and many fantastic care workers. The failings of a few smear the rest. But we do need to talk about it when it goes wrong. Lack of dignity is the thing that's most commonly reported to us, and after a point this becomes abuse. To tackle the issues we need to be comfortable talking about it and create an environment in which elderly people feel supported. And we need to give dignity back to care workers – if they are undervalued it becomes difficult to do the job. And we must remind people that it's a real life issue. We must be absolutely clear that it is as unacceptable as child abuse.

### Christopher Manthorp
*Society Guardian columnist and director of older people's services for Epic, part of Circle Anglia Group*

I have worked in residential care for older people for much of my working life and have always believed that good homes are one of the best options available to the really vulnerable – the very frail and people with dementia, for example. It's impossible to deny that abuse does take place – we have occasional prosecutions to prove it

– but the scale is tiny. Exaggeration contributes to giving residential care an image problem it doesn't deserve. The sector is improving steadily. The Commission for Social Care Inspection (CSCI) has had an enormous and very largely positive impact on standards, concentrating heavily on nutrition, for example. It does the government little credit to preside over the effective dissolution of CSCI [it becomes part of the new Care Quality Commission later this year] yet to do so little to tackle the appalling and notorious ageism that characterises the health system in the UK, or the genuinely malnourished allocation of resources to older people in this country.

### Paul Burstow
*Liberal Democrat MP for Sutton and Cheam, and co-chair of the all-party group on ageing and older people*

From this government the study is the modern day equivalent of Nero fiddling while Rome burned. What is required now is tough action to put abusive homes out of business, and police action to put the worst offenders behind bars. In a debate in parliament yesterday, I pointed out that the law is being broken every day by GPs who prescribe and care home staff who administer antipsychotic drugs to older people with dementia to keep them quiet and manageable – it is chemical restraint. The evidence is clear: these drugs shorten lives, increase the risk of stroke and have other harmful side-effects. It is time their use was routinely reviewed and banned in all but the most severe cases of dementia. The national dementia strategy must deliver dignity and end the scandal of abusive prescribing.

*For more on older people at risk of abuse in institutional care go to SocietyGuardian. co.uk/longtermcare*

*2 April 2008*

# Loneliness a major worry

**Fear of being alone is major source of anxiety as we grow old, according to a new survey**

Isolation and lack of contact with friends and family in old age is seen as a greater worry than concerns about declining health or finances.

elderlyparents.org.uk – an organisation which provides free advice to children coping with the demands of ageing parents – found that nearly half of those questioned said being lonely was their main concern in the future.

A third of respondents said securing their home against intruders was a priority. One in five remain anxious about managing household chores while five per cent feared being unable to contact anyone in an emergency.

Mike Bingham of elderlyparents.org.uk said: 'Traditionally worries about health and maintaining independence are seen as the main concerns, but it appears the next generation of older people will be just as concerned with their emotional well-being as their health.

'This will heap huge pressure on the so-called Sandwich Generation, those people coping with the demands of elderly parents and their own children.

'Feeling guilty about not spending enough time with their elderly relatives is just one more thing for them to worry about.'

The findings painted a bleak picture of life for Britain's pensioners, with an estimated 300,000 saying they often go an entire month without speaking to family or neighbours.

Mr Bingham added: 'It is a fairly depressing picture but it is important to know that there is help and support for people looking after elderly parents.

'That can mean anything from arranging for private home visits for your parents or something as simple as getting them online, where they can talk to other people in chat rooms.'

⇨ Information from Saga. Visit www.saga.co.uk for more information.

# Prevalence of elder abuse

## Comic Relief research shows numbers of older people abused at home

New research, revealing the true extent of abuse suffered by older people in the UK, was released today by Comic Relief Chief Executive, Kevin Cahill, and Health Minster, Ivan Lewis.

The UK Study of Abuse and Neglect, carried out over two years by independent researchers at National Centre for Social Research and Kings College, London, was based on a survey of around 2000 people aged 66 and over who live in their own homes (including sheltered housing).

The findings of the study show that:

⇨ 2.6% or 227,000 people were neglected or abused by family, close friends and care workers in the last year; and

⇨ 4% or 342,400 people were neglected or abused in the last year by family, close friends and care workers, neighbours and acquaintances (i.e. a broader definition of those who might abuse).

⇨ Mistreatment is broken down into neglect (1.1%), financial abuse (0.7%), psychological and physical abuse (both 0.4%) and sexual abuse (0.2%).

⇨ The majority of the incidents involved a partner (51%) or another family member (49%) followed by a voluntary or paid care worker (13%) and close friend (5%).

Kevin Cahill, CEO, Comic Relief, said:

'Comic Relief feels passionately that growing older with dignity, free from abuse, is something we should all expect rather than aspire to. Using some of the money raised through Red Nose Day we have taken the lead in funding this research and over the years, through appeal films and the BBC One drama *Dad* we have helped raise awareness of this enormous social issue.

'Thousands of older people are suffering abuse and this robust research means we can no longer deny that society's attitude towards older people is a problem.

'Now that we have achieved this first step these figures need to be used positively so decision makers and care givers can ensure that if anyone faces abuse they can get access to services and receive the help they need.

'People are living longer and the numbers of older people are set to rise in the following decades.

'This is the first time Comic Relief has funded research, and from the findings we hope we have provided the evidence to effect change.'

Care Services Minister, Ivan Lewis, said:

'This research gives us the first objective and scientific assessment of the prevalence of elder abuse. We now have with some precision an up-to-date estimate of the size of the challenge that we face. Older people deserve to be treated with dignity and respect – abuse in any setting is just unacceptable.

'I want people to be as outraged by the abuse of an older person as they are by the abuse of a child. Sadly, we are nowhere near that yet as a society but that culture has to change.

'This research shows us the nature of the problems that we will all face in the future.

'That's why today I'm announcing two measures for the first time, national and local records on the abuse of older people will be systematically collected so that each individual council can monitor abuse locally and act on it.

'It is essential to put in place the mechanisms for collecting accurate and impartial data that will allow help to be targeted where it is most needed. Knowing the size of the challenge nationally is one thing but each individual council ought equally to know what's going on locally. A systematic data collection will identify this and allow comparisons between councils.

'No Secrets is the existing guidance on safeguarding vulnerable adults, launched in 2000. The aim of No Secrets is to ensure that health, social services and the police, are able to work together to protect vulnerable adults from abuse.

'Seven years on, and in the light of several serious incidences of adult abuse, it is timely to review this guidance and to consult with other government departments that have an interest in this field. New guidance is necessary to reflect the evidence in today's report and respond to the new demographic realities which are affecting our society. We will also consider the case for legislation as part of the review process.'

*14 June 2007*

⇨ The above information is reprinted with kind permission from the Department of Health. Visit www.dh.gov.uk for more information.

© Crown copyright

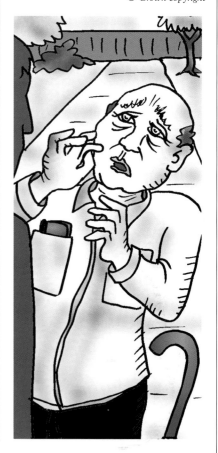

# Retirees spending freely

## Information from the Economic and Social Research Council

**A**s the 'baby boomer' generation begins to join the ranks of the retired so policy makers must a fresh look at their behaviour as consumers, says a new study funded by the Economic and Social Research Council.

Far from being simply media creations, it seems that the caricatures of 'silver surfers' and 'Saga-louts' have some basis in truth as the lives of older people increasingly mirror those of the rest of society in terms of their spending and leisure activities.

'From passive to active consumers: ageing and consumption in Britain 1963-1998' – research based on an analysis of the Family Expenditure Survey (FES) – compared how people's spending on goods and services as well as household income has changed over time.

Dr Paul Higgs, from University College London, who led the research, explained: 'Preceding studies have neglected the changing cultural context of the consumption patterns of older people, and so we wanted to see how they had participated in consumer society.'

The study explored expenditure patterns by retired households, with particular emphasis on food, fuel, alcohol, clothing and household goods. Results suggest that retired households do not now differ greatly from each other in their expenditure, despite some variations based on income.

Overall, successive generations of retirees have increased their consumption of goods with, for example, later generations spending more on leisure activities such as holidays.

According to Dr Higgs, most retired households are now participating as contemporary consumers. He explained: 'Those retiring today

E·S·R·C
ECONOMIC
& SOCIAL
RESEARCH
COUNCIL

helped pioneer the creation of the post-war consumer culture – young people in the 50s, 60s and 70s had more money than previous generations and an increasing range of things to spend it on. We believe that this experience has informed the way they behave in retirement, with recent retirees strongly defined by the impact of consumer society on their lives and expectations.'

---

**The lives of older people increasingly mirror those of the rest of society in terms of their spending and leisure activities**

---

All income groups spent less on food – down from just under a third to just over a quarter of total expenditure – whilst spending on household goods rose from around four to just under 10 per cent. Spending on fuel was reduced, while that on alcohol and clothing remained broadly similar.

Researchers also compared patterns of ownership of selected consumer goods amongst the retired population compared to

the employed and unemployed, and found that patterns had converged over time. Whereas the spending habits of these different groups was distinct in the 1960s, ownership of telephones, televisions and fridge/freezers, for example, have since increased and evened out. Ownership of newer household goods such as microwave ovens and VCRs showed similar patterns over much shorter periods of time, with clear differences in 1993 narrowing by 2001.

However, the research also highlighted that whilst levels of washing machine and PC ownership had risen for all groups, the retired and unemployed continued to lag behind the employed. Less than two per cent of retired households owned a PC in 1993, and whilst this figure had risen tenfold by 2001, PC ownership in employed households more than doubled to over half during the same period.

*14 December 2007*

⇨ The above information is reprinted with kind permission from the Economic and Social Research Council. Visit www.esrc.ac.uk for more information.

© ESRC

*Less than two per cent of retired households owned a PC in 1993: this figure had risen tenfold by 2001*

# Life begins at 55

## Financial freedom begins in the mid-fifties according to Birmingham Midshires' latest Life 2 report

The saying goes that life begins at 40, but this well-known adage is actually 15 years off the truth, according to a new report out today from Birmingham Midshires, a leading savings provider in the UK.

> **More than half of respondents (55 per cent) in their early 50s are still working the nine-to-five grind, whilst 23 per cent of those aged over 55 have given up full-time work**

Birmingham Midshires' Life 2 campaign, which explores issues affecting the over-50s, has found that 55 is the age at which people discover their financial freedom and embark on their second life, free from some of their most pressing financial strains.

When quizzed on the financial burden posed by children, Birmingham Midshires found that, in their early 50s, almost a half (47 per cent) of the respondents still have children living at home and are still supporting them financially (49 per cent). Past the age of 55, however, just one in six of respondents have children still living under the same roof and three-quarters no longer need to provide financial handouts to their offspring.

Shaking off mortgage responsibilities also starts at the age of 55. Birmingham Midshires' figures reveal that while 41 per cent of those in their early 50s are still saddled with a mortgage, this figure halves to one in five (22 per cent) of those aged 55 and over.

Furthermore, more than half of respondents (55 per cent) in their early 50s are still working the nine-to-five grind, whilst 23 per cent of those aged over 55 have given up full-time work.

Jason Robinson, Director of Savings Operations at Birmingham Midshires, commented on the findings: 'After years of bringing up children and working hard, those in their 50s can look forward to a more relaxing way of life, with fewer financial strains.

'The saying goes that life begins at 40 but it is interesting to see our research indicates otherwise. This could be down to a number of economic and social factors, such as rising house prices and people having children later in life, all of which take their toll on the age of financial independence.'
*23 August 2007*

⇨ The above information is reprinted with kind permission from Birmingham Midshires. Visit www.askbm.co.uk for more information.
© *Birmingham Midshires*

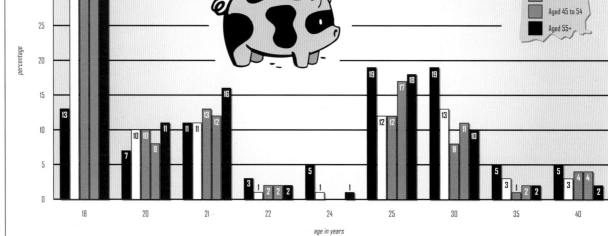

**Saving for retirement**

Respondents were asked: 'At what age do you think people need to start to save for their retirement?'. Results by age group.

Legend: Aged 18 to 24, Aged 25 to 34, Aged 35 to 44, Aged 45 to 54, Aged 55+

Sample size: 1956. Fieldwork: 28 December 2007 to 3 January 2008. Source: YouGov 2008 (www.yougov.com).

# Aim high, save low

## Poll reveals regional gaps in young people's plans and funds for later life

Far from retiring quietly, young people today expect to be able to afford the things they enjoy now when they retire with foreign holidays, satellite TV and gym membership as standard. With over half the nation's under 34-year-olds not saving anything at all, they are at risk of becoming the 'big dreams, small assets' generation.

Young people in the South West are on track for a bigger shock than others across the UK if they don't start saving for their retirement soon, followed closely by Scotland and the West Midlands. Even in Tyne Tees, where people are most realistic, there's still a large gap between plans and funds for later life with the Welsh hot on their heels.

A YouGov poll of nearly 2,000 people from across the UK revealed young people are failing to back their plans with hard cash.

Commenting on the survey, Paul Banfield of Best Advice Financial Planning Ltd said:

'It's great that young people want more and the message to them is simple – you can take steps today to set yourself up for the kind of life you want tomorrow. If you don't wake up to this opportunity and simply cruise towards retirement with your eyes closed, you may have a rude awakening.'

### Greatest expectations

Young people in Scotland are most likely to believe they can afford their current lifestyles when they stop work compared to just over a third in Tyne Tees.

### Sleepiest savers

Two-thirds of young people in the South West haven't started saving followed by just over half of people from the West Midlands and the North West. People in Wales are best at putting cash aside but still a third are not saving anything by the age of 34.

Pensions Minister Mike O'Brien added:

'Work and saving should go hand in hand. Pensions aren't just for pensioners, they are a young person's issue. If young people don't have a save-now attitude they could miss a trick. Pension pounds work harder the earlier you save – a £1 saved at 20 could be worth up to sixty per cent more at retirement than the same £1 saved at 40.'

*12 February 2008*

⇨ The above information is reprinted with kind permission from the Department for Work and Pensions. Visit www.dwp.gov.uk for more information.

© *Crown copyright*

## Heading for a shock

Topping the chart with their heads in the clouds are young people in the South West, followed by the Scots.

**1** South West – biggest expectation/saving gap
**2** Scotland
**3** West Midlands
**4** South East
**5** East Midlands
**6** North West
**7** Yorkshire
**8** London
**9** Wales
**10** Tyne Tees

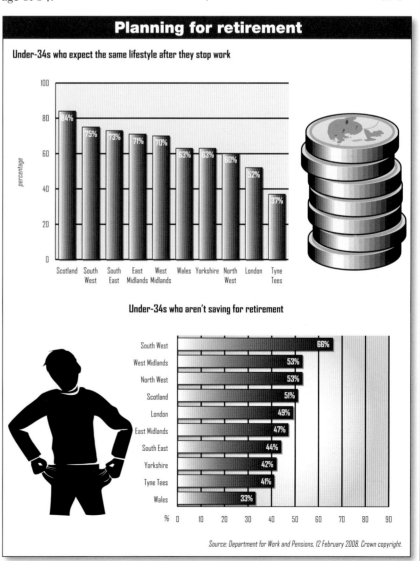

### Planning for retirement

Under-34s who expect the same lifestyle after they stop work

| Region | percentage |
|---|---|
| Scotland | 84% |
| South West | 75% |
| South East | 73% |
| East Midlands | 71% |
| West Midlands | 70% |
| Wales | 63% |
| Yorkshire | 63% |
| North West | 60% |
| London | 52% |
| Tyne Tees | 37% |

Under-34s who aren't saving for retirement

| Region | % |
|---|---|
| South West | 66% |
| West Midlands | 53% |
| North West | 53% |
| Scotland | 51% |
| London | 49% |
| East Midlands | 47% |
| South East | 44% |
| Yorkshire | 42% |
| Tyne Tees | 41% |
| Wales | 33% |

Source: Department for Work and Pensions, 12 February 2008. Crown copyright.

# Next generation of Brits facing bleak future

## Supporting parents and own kids is 'savings gap' Brits' biggest financial fear

**B**ritain's pension crisis is set to escalate, a new study warns today, with a generation of adults facing the triple pressure of the financial 'hat trick' scenario of supporting both their parents and their own children, whilst having no financial plans to safeguard their own future either.

The Norwich Union study reveals one in three Brits most dread the possibility of simultaneously financing both their children and their parents.

A further six in ten (59 per cent) over-50s admit their pensions and savings are unlikely to see them through retirement – leading over half (51 per cent) of adult children to fear the knock-on effect on their own financial futures.

One in four (28 per cent) adult children are ready to cash in their savings and investments to fund their parents' retirement, while others consider taking their parents to live with them (24 per cent) and a fifth (21 per cent) would change their own lifestyles to find extra money.

Scott Brown, Norwich Union spokesperson, says: 'Talk of the so-called "savings gap" is nothing new – but this study is an urgent reminder of the very real impact this issue could have on the next generation of retirees.

'What makes it all the more alarming, however, is that, while adult children told us they fear supporting their own parents, an incredible two-thirds (63 per cent) admitted they have no financial plans for their own retirement.'

Two in five (43%) adult children suspect their parents might struggle financially in retirement and are concerned that the impact on their own lives will see them:

⇨ losing their own savings (45 per cent);
⇨ having to work longer than they had planned (37 per cent);
⇨ not being able to send their children to university (25 per cent);
⇨ having to radically downsize their own lifestyles (24 per cent).

But they refuse to broach the issue with their parents. Almost half (48 per cent) have no idea how their parents plan to fund their retirement – and six in ten (61%) say they could not imagine talking to their parents about their finances.

Scott Brown, of Norwich Union, said: 'Unless we tackle this now, we face a never-ending cycle of financial struggle.

'The first step is simply for families to talk about their finances together and break this taboo.'

Norwich Union has created a five-point plan to help families talk about financial planning:

1 Communicate. Get a grip on your family's financial situation and get your head out of the sand today. Ignoring the problem won't make it go away; it will just make it worse. It can be difficult to talk about money, especially with loved ones, but by being open and honest now you can help to avoid the burden of debt and stress later in life.

2 Remember you are not alone. Everyone needs to plan for their retirement, no matter what their age. People are living longer and healthier lives, so it's even more important to think about how and when you and your family can save for retirement.

3 Plan ahead. With a bit of planning, you can do a lot to help your family get ready for retirement. Fairly small changes now can make a big difference to your family's lives in the future – and you don't need to blow your monthly budget.

4 Money-saving options. Pensions can be confusing and many people don't know where to begin, especially when there are so many other things to spend your money on. But the truth is that a pension is one of the most effective ways to invest for your retirement because you can get tax relief on the money you save in a pension scheme. If you're a parent don't be afraid to sit down and talk through your pension plans with your children, that way they will know what to expect and you'll avoid any surprises later in life.

5 Ask the experts. There are lots of organisations out there who can help. Don't struggle on your own, as a family you should collectively seek professional advice.

*12 February 2008*

⇨ The above information is reprinted with kind permission from Norwich Union. Visit www.norwichunion.com for more information.

*© Norwich Union*

# Pensions Act 2007

## Huge boost for women and carers as Pensions Act 2007 becomes law

Women and carers received a huge boost today thanks to the reforms to the state pension system in the Pensions Act 2007, which has received Royal Assent.

For many low-income women, this could mean an extra £50 a week by the 2050s from the state pension.

Secretary of State for Work and Pensions Peter Hain said: 'This Act will deliver the most important reforms to the state pension system in generations.

'Many women and carers are currently denied a full pension entitlement because their family and caring responsibilities mean they are not in work long enough to qualify.

> ## 'Many women and carers are currently denied a full pension entitlement because their family and caring responsibilities mean they are not in work long enough to qualify'

'This Act provides women and carers with a fair deal, making it easier to balance their responsibilities and recognising their contribution to society as a whole.

'Around three-quarters of women retiring in 2010 will be entitled to a full Basic State Pension – compared with 35 per cent now, and 50 per cent without reform. More than 90 per cent of women and men retiring in 2025 will be entitled to a full Basic State Pension.'

The number of years' contributions required to achieve a full Basic State Pension will be reduced to 30 for women and men from April 6, 2010. The current requirement is 39 years for women and 44 for men. The Act will

gradually increase State Pension Age to 68 by 2046 for men and women.

The Act lays the foundations for the new pensions settlement being introduced by the Government. As well as providing a boost for women and carers, the Act re-links the Basic State Pension with earnings from 2012, or by the end of the next Parliament, and provides for a simpler flat-rate State Second Pension.

Hailing the new pensions settlement, Peter Hain said:

'This Act lays the foundation for the new pensions settlement. By re-linking the Basic State Pension with earnings, we will ensure that living standards for older people keep pace with the rest of society. And by providing a fairer deal on state pensions, we are providing a platform for greater saving by both individuals and employers in the new savings scheme we are introducing in the next Pensions Bill. For the first time, all employees will have access to a workplace

pension with a minimum employer contribution, and a contribution from the Government.'

He added:

'It is a tribute to the consensus we've built that there is now widespread agreement that people will need to work longer in the future – it would be wrong to leave it to future generations to foot the bill for people living longer.

'Maintaining that consensus is essential if we are to build the highest possible public confidence in the new pensions settlement and to ensure that it lasts for the generations to come.'

The announcement of Royal Assent was made this afternoon.
*26 July 2007*

⇨ The above information is reprinted with kind permission from the Department for Work and Pensions. Visit www.dwp.gov.uk for more information.

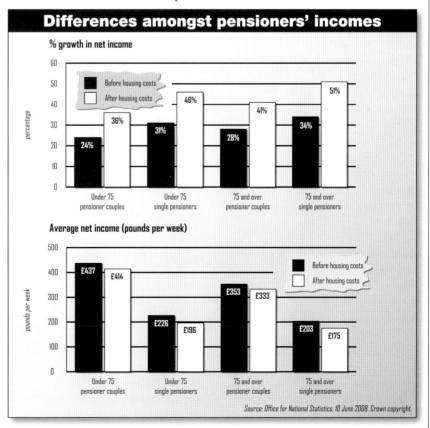

**Differences amongst pensioners' incomes**

*% growth in net income*

Before housing costs / After housing costs

Under 75 pensioner couples: 24% / 36%
Under 75 single pensioners: 31% / 46%
75 and over pensioner couples: 28% / 41%
75 and over single pensioners: 34% / 51%

**Average net income (pounds per week)**

Before housing costs / After housing costs

Under 75 pensioner couples: £437 / £414
Under 75 single pensioners: £226 / £196
75 and over pensioner couples: £353 / £333
75 and over single pensioners: £203 / £175

Source: Office for National Statistics, 10 June 2008. Crown copyright.

# Pension could protect world's poorest

## Older people in developing countries among those hit hardest by recent rises in food prices

HelpAge International, the global network promoting and protecting the rights of disadvantaged older people, has today renewed its call for the introduction of a universal social pension in the wake of rising food prices that are currently affecting the world's poorest people.

> **100 million older people in developing countries who live without a regular income on less than $1 a day are among those hit hardest by the recent rises**

The EU Development Commissioner Louis Michel said earlier this week that the rising costs could lead to a humanitarian crisis in Africa. British Prime Minister Gordon Brown today warned that the cost of food was threatening to roll back progress made on development.

100 million older people in developing countries who live without a regular income on less than $1 a day are among those hit hardest by the recent rises, largest in foods such as rice, wheat flour and maize. In much of West Africa, the price of rice has risen by 50 per cent. Food riots have taken place in countries including Senegal, Mozambique, and Cameroon.

HelpAge International is calling for the introduction of a universal social pension for people over the age of 60 which will increase food security and nutritional intake for older people, ensuring that they are less vulnerable to sudden rises in the cost of food. Many older people also support younger generations of family within their households, particularly through the provision of care to grandchildren orphaned by HIV/AIDS, making the need for food security even greater.

Evidence from developing countries indicates that older recipients of regular cash transfers such as pensions spend it on their own or their families' immediate needs, including food and healthcare, and on investments such as livestock which serve as a form of security in times of need.

The old age pension in Lesotho, launched in 2004, has significantly improved food security by increasing food consumption, stabilising access to food, and improving nutrition through the purchase of more nutritious food such as meat. In South Africa, social pensions increase the income of the poorest 5 per cent of the population by 50 per cent.

Pensions can also help to stimulate local economies and encourage sustainable food production.

HelpAge International is currently working in close collaboration with the Commission of Social Affairs of the African Union (AU) to deliver a series of national consultations and regional expert meetings on approaches to extending social protection, including through social pensions, in advance of the first ever AU Conference of Social Development Ministers to be held later this year. The first regional expert meeting is to be held in Uganda between 28 and 30 April 2008.

Richard Blewitt, Chief Executive of HelpAge International, says: 'It is a scandal that 80 per cent of the world's people have no access to social security, many of them older people who are particularly affected at times like these. There is a great opportunity to address this through social pensions and many good models exist from Bolivia to Nepal and Lesotho.'

Amleset Tewodros, Regional Programmes Manager for Africa at HelpAge International, says: 'In a world which is capable of producing enough to feed everyone, universal social pensions guarantee that older people and multigenerational households are able to afford the basic minimum diet they require, and can plan ahead to meet challenges such as rising food prices.'
*10 April 2008*

⇨ The above information is reprinted with kind permission from HelpAge International. Visit www. helpage.org for more information.
*© HelpAge International*

# UK state pension is 'worst in Europe'

**By Hilary Osborne and agencies**

The UK's state pension system has been rated the worst in Europe for the second year running in a report published today.

Research by employee benefits firm Aon Consulting showed that an average earner retiring this year would receive a pension worth just 17% of their salary, compared with an EU average of 57%.

Even in the Netherlands, which is the country with the second lowest payment, the state pension is worth 30% of the average retiree's salary – almost twice the figure in the UK.

Aon said 'the inadequacy of the state system' was 'beyond question', with only the lowest earners being entitled to anything near the pensions offered in other countries.

A gradual shift away from the state towards employers and individuals meant the UK had the largest funded private pension system in Europe, but mis-selling scandals and rule changes had knocked confidence, Aon said.

Donald Duval, chief actuary at Aon Consulting UK, said: 'More needs to be done to restore confidence in private schemes so as to drive an increased level of contributions – people cannot afford to rely on the state pension, which remains the lowest in Europe.'

The report, which compared the pension systems in 25 of the EU's 27 member states, found the UK was one of only seven countries where the spend on state pensions was likely to remain below 10% of GDP.

However, Aon also said the government's plans to introduce personal accounts, which will see employees automatically enrolled on to pension schemes and employers making compulsory contributions, would increase private pension coverage and counter a fall in the number of final salary schemes on offer.

It added that analysis of the private pension system, affordability of providing state pensions and the UK's demographics, where the average retirement age of 62.6 years is among the highest in Europe, put the UK's pension in fifth place overall.

## Ageing population pressures

Top of the firm's third annual Pensions Barometer was Denmark, which also topped the table last year.

The country's state pension scheme offers a 75% salary replacement for the average earner, while low earners get a pension worth 120% of their working salary, meaning they effectively get a pay rise when they retire.

Life expectancy in Denmark is relatively low, at 81 years, which eases the pressure on the state scheme.

'In Europe, the countries with the worst problems tend to be those where the average retirement age is low and they face major demographic and social security issues, which if not addressed will create unsustainable pension systems,' said Duvall.

'The rising pressure an ageing population is placing on government expenditure can be mitigated by governments encouraging greater use of funded pensions, which mean that today's workers pay for their own pensions instead of relying on the next generation to do so.'

The pensions reform minister, Mike O'Brien, said the UK's pension system was different from other countries' and it was 'misleading' to look at the state pension in isolation.

'In the UK we are reforming the system to make the state pension simpler, fairer for women and carers, and more generous, whilst remaining affordable,' said O'Brien.

'Proposals in the next pensions bill, later this year, will make it easier for millions of people to save to meet their retirement aspirations through automatic enrolment into a qualifying workplace scheme or personal accounts.'

Changes in the UK pension system, including raising the state pension age to 68 by 2046, are currently going through parliament.

Yesterday, the Pensions Policy Institute said the government should rethink its plans for personal accounts and allow savers to build a fund of £6,000 in a pension without losing means-tested benefits.

*13 November 2007*

© *Guardian Newspapers Limited 2008*

I used to work for peanuts... Now I just feed them to the birds!

# Charging into poverty

## Care charges risk leading older and disabled people into poverty, says new report

Rising care charges are putting older and disabled people at risk of not being able to afford to eat, heat their homes, wash or get essential support, says a new report published today (4 June) by the Coalition on Charging.

The report is backed by 18 major organisations that form the Coalition – representing disabled people, older people, people with long-term health conditions and carers.

Based on a snapshot survey, the report, *Charging into poverty?*, reveals that rising charges for people to receive care in their own homes, are causing disabled and older people in England to reduce or even stop their support services.

---

**80% of people surveyed who no longer use care services say the charges contributed to their decision to stop their support**

---

The survey found that:
⇨ 80% of people surveyed who no longer use care services say the charges contributed to their decision to stop their support.
⇨ A fifth (22%) of people surveyed who are currently using support suggested they would stop if charges increased further.
⇨ 29% of respondents do not feel their essential expenditure (related to impairment/health condition) is taken into account in financial assessments to pay charges.
⇨ Nearly three-quarters (72%) of people surveyed believe the Government should think about the charges people pay for support at home in adult care reform plans.

Since 1948 local authorities have been able to charge for care and support provided to help people remain living in their own home. Charging for care and support at home has become more common since the introduction of Community Care reforms in the early 1990s.

Responses to the survey show strong feelings of despair at the current situation and anxiety for the future:

'I have a disability with which I was born. Perhaps the Government might consider...other areas before taking money from the most vulnerable members of society who are already living in the poverty zone.'

Imelda Redmond, Chief Executive of Carers UK, says:

'Local councils must understand the terrible impact that their inconsistent charging regimes have on the lives of disabled people, their families and carers. This report backs up what carers have told us over the last year during our consultation for the National Carers Strategy.

'At a national level we will be pushing the Government to include a thorough analysis of the impact of charging as part of its review of care and support services and the forthcoming Green Paper.'

Sue Bott, Chair of the Coalition on Charging and NCIL Director, says:

'Restricted access to social services and increased charges for support has had a huge impact on the day-to-day lives of disabled people, older people and their families. The shocking reality is that people needing support are being forced to choose between eating properly and using vital care services.

'The government must conduct a thorough review to fully understand the damage that rising care charges are having on people's lives and ensure the care reform green paper delivers a framework which ends the choice of food or care.'

In May 2008 the Government launched a national debate on adult care reform in England in advance of a green paper. The Coalition on Charging is calling on Government to conduct a thorough review of the impact of care charges to be undertaken from 2008, and for these issues to be addressed in adult care reform in England.
*4 June 2008*

⇨ The above information is reprinted with kind permission from Carers UK. Visit www.carersuk.org for more information.

© Carers UK

# Care homes

## Information from Help the Aged

Care homes are undervalued and struggling. Older people face uncertainty about how they will be cared for, and who will pay for it.

### What we want

We believe that there is a mismatch of affordable, quality care home places available to meet the need and that older people's choice is being eroded. The problems are as follows:

⇨ Erosion of choice – Older people are being steered away from care homes as they are viewed as a care option of 'last resort' rather than a positive choice.

⇨ Unfair – The UK Government wants older people to be cared for in their own homes, but inadequate funding for social care is failing to give them the companionship and security they need. With ever competing priorities, older people always come last in the funding queue.

---

## The care home struggle is robbing older people of their dignity and choice

---

⇨ Erratic quality care – Care homes struggle to provide good quality care: a dwindling workforce, increasing costs and a poor image all mean that successful care homes should be championed.

### Erosion of choice

Although most people prefer to remain in their own home as they grow older, they don't want to live out their lives in isolation, anxiety and neglect. There are a number of people who require a level of care, companionship and peace of mind that they can only receive in a good care home. Admissions to care homes usually happen at times of crisis. If seen as a positive option, with preparation and

planning, residents in care homes are more likely to enjoy quality care that allows them to stay active and involved in their community, which we believe is their right.

But care homes are struggling in the UK. Increasingly complex funding issues and demands on proprietors are making it hard to keep going whilst barriers such as planning permission limit their ability to diversify.

That means older people can't get the quality care they need. They have to pay more and have less choice over where they spend the last years of their life. The care home struggle is robbing older people of their dignity and choice.

### Unfair

There is a disparity between those older people who can afford to pay for their own care, and those whose care is funded by the State. Care home owners receive more money from self-funders, who are inadvertently subsidising those funded by the state. Families and charities are often having to make up funding shortfalls of up to £100 a week for older people's care.

Older people who rely on State funding often have little choice about where they end up, or the kind of care they receive. If care home places exist, the UK Government says older people

should have a choice. But the reality is there are so few places, there's really no choice at all. Some older people say they feel pressured, bullied and hurried into making decisions. Many become stuck in the system waiting for funding to be available.

Shouldn't all of us be able to choose where we live and have the time to make informed choices?

### Erratic quality care

The care home sector is fragmented. Some care homes deliver a high standard of individual care where people feel secure and part of a small community. But many older people suffer in care homes that are isolated themselves from the mainstream health and social care services, and need updating to meet 21st-century demands.

It is time for a fundamental shift in attitudes to older people and their care. The system itself, based on the Poor Law, is too rigid and is out of date to meet current and future needs. Such a change is daunting, but let's look at what works for older people now and replicate it. Help the Aged welcomes the review of social care funding undertaken by Sir Derek Wanless on behalf of the Kings Fund in 2006. The evidence has confirmed the need for much more money. We urge the UK Government to address the findings of this crucial report before it is too late. We insist on a public debate to discuss changing attitudes to older people and how the money can be found for their care.

Older people should be allowed and empowered to choose their own care home and care package if they wish. That means more quality care homes are needed, and the Direct Payments system (which provides older people with money to spend on their own care) should be made more accessible.

### Frequently asked questions

*Why are there so many problems in the care home sector?*
Society's attitude to older people, and the value we place on our elders, is reflected by the poor quality of the services we offer them. Help the Aged believes people's worth and individuality should not diminish as they reach the end of their lives and we urge you to consider what might be the best ways to fund the care needed.

*What is Help the Aged doing?*
Having campaigned for the need for the proper funding and planning of long-term care we welcome the Kings Fund's review of the funding of long-term care. We are now focusing on a major programme in partnership with the National Care Forum on the Quality of Life in Care Homes.

This is about valuing those who live and work in care homes and bringing in the sector to the mainstream health and social care system. It is research-based and is designed to involve older people and all those in the sector from care staff to commissioners and inspectors to practically make life better, more meaningful and satisfying for the care home population

*Where can I get more information on paying for care?*
The Help the Aged Care Fees Advice service can offer advice and support on meeting the cost of care. Specialist advisers provide free, impartial financial advice, helping older people to find the best ways to pay for care.

⇨ The above information is reprinted with kind permission from Help the Aged. Visit www.helptheaged.org.uk for more information.

*© Help the Aged*

# Huge public worries about quality of care

## Bleak expectations of care in Britain revealed by Age Concern

**E**ight out of ten people in Britain are very concerned about the quality of care they or their loved ones will get in later life, research for Age Concern reveals today. Four out of ten people are not even confident they will be treated with dignity or respect, despite a high profile Government campaign to address this.

The charity is launching a major new campaign – 'The Big Q' – challenging all the party leaders to match their rhetoric with a commitment to radical reform to improve the quality of care, ahead of a public consultation the Government is planning to hold later this year.

Polling carried out for Age Concern found that people of all ages and incomes are deeply concerned about the quality of the personal care they would get if they need help with everyday tasks like getting out of bed, washing, dressing or taking medication. The charity described the findings as further evidence of how the care system is routinely failing older people and their families.

The poll shows that our worries about the quality of personal care increase with age. Seven out of ten young adults (18- to 34-year-olds) are very concerned about the quality of personal care that a loved one or they themselves would get. This rises to nine out of ten people aged 75 or older, by which time they are more likely to need some help or to know people who do.

Gordon Lishman, Director General of Age Concern, said: 'People are fed up with fighting to get the care they need in later life, either for themselves or for their loved ones. The care system clearly isn't working, which is why radical reform is urgently needed. The Government urgently needs to set a timetable for change, so that people can be sure they are not being fobbed off.'

The charity's campaign – 'The Big Q' – sets out five building blocks for the foundation of a new quality care system in its new report *Quality not Inequality*:
⇨ Respecting people's dignity.
⇨ Enabling people to maintain their independence.
⇨ Ensuring fairness for all who need care
⇨ Giving clarity about getting the support you need.
⇨ Increasing the amount of money available to provide quality care.

Age Concern will be holding its own consultation events up and down the country which will challenge councillors and politicians to listen and act on the views of local people.
*28 April 2008*

⇨ The above information is reprinted with kind permission from Age Concern. Visit www.ageconcern.org.uk for more information.

*© Age Concern*

# Funding long-term care

## Families in the dark when it comes to funding long-term care for their loved ones

> ⇨ *43 per cent of adults over 50 who have put others into care did not seek funding advice.*
> ⇨ *Of those that have, one in three sought advice from doctors and nurses.*
> ⇨ *Only 12 per cent consulted an independent financial adviser (IFA).*

**N**ew research released today by Partnership – one of the UK's leading providers of ill-health retirement and care solutions – reveals that more than a third (37 per cent) of British adults over 50 have had to put someone into residential care. Of them, almost half (43 per cent) did not seek any advice when making this difficult decision. In particular, this leaves the 59 per cent of families that the research shows rely on local authority funding financially at risk – especially as qualifying for this type of funding becomes harder and care home costs escalate – leaving them to fall back on hard-earned savings or the sale of the family home.

---

**More than a third (37 per cent) of British adults over 50 have had to put someone into residential care**

---

The study identifies that people don't know where to turn for advice in this critical area and are therefore leaving themselves financially exposed to an unknown cost. Partnership is calling for financial advisers and providers to help raise awareness of both the entitlements and the funding options available in this complex and sensitive market.

Partnership's study shows that even those who do look for advice are unnecessarily gambling with their financial future by seeking it from inappropriate sources. Most people (66 per cent) go to their local authorities for advice, where staff are not qualified to provide full financial advice, or may even be pointing people in the wrong direction. Others undertake their own 'DIY' internet research or seek advice from friends (16 and 13 per cent respectively), while only 12 per cent consult an IFA (12 per cent). A third of people (34 per cent) rely on the medical profession – local GPs and nurses – to advise on how best to pay for any care.

Ian Owen, Chairman of Partner-ship, comments: 'With an ageing population, the number of people having to make crucial decisions about their loved ones' welfare is increasing. And with the pressure on local authorities to control their costs forcing more people to fund the care themselves, the lack of knowledge about entitlements, funding choices, the costs associated with care homes and the probability of investments being exhausted is a major worry for thousands of families and carers.

'The flip-side of this is an untapped market for advice on long-term care which the financial services industry is failing to address.'

A decrease in government support and rapidly rising care home costs make it increasingly necessary for people to fund care privately. The estimated market for private long-term care is around £3.5 billion and growing, yet in 2006 only 3000 highly tax efficient long-term care annuity products were sold. This represents a huge – currently unrealised – opportunity for IFAs and providers. Moreover, with full-time care in a home costing around £25,000 to £30,000 a year – and even more if nursing care is needed – informed decisions are essential if people are to avoid serious financial problems in the future.

Ian Owen continues: 'This market is one where advisers can really make a positive difference to the lives of thousands of people. State-funded care is disappearing for all but the most needy and any future Government-led developments are likely to involve some form of funding partnership between the state and the individual.

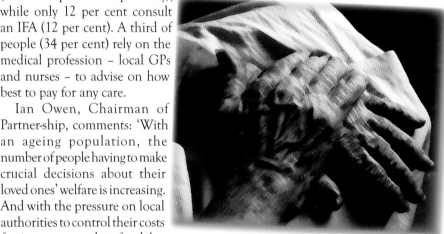

'We would encourage IFAs to step into the breach and meet this very real need – most of us know at least one person who has had to put someone into a care home and has probably exposed themselves to avoidable financial risks in so doing.

'We would also encourage every adviser to take CF8 [a course providing a knowledge of long-term care insurance] to enable them to give the fullest level of advice and information to their clients and their families, and remove some of their anxiety at what can be an extremely difficult time.'
*17 November 2007*

⇨ The above information is reprinted with kind permission from Partnership. Visit www.partnership.co.uk for more information.

*© Partnership*

# Out of sight, out of mind

## Social exclusion in later life: summary, solutions and recommendations

### What is social exclusion?

Social exclusion is policymakers' jargon for being cut off from the mainstream of society. It's an impassive term but one that captures the important truth that disadvantage is not just about being poor. Being socially excluded means being unable to access the things in life that most of society takes for granted – like a properly equipped, well-maintained home; close friends and regular company; stimulating activity; and easy access to important services such as GPs, shops and post offices.

---

**56% of severely excluded people over 50 do not consider their health to be good, compared to just 17% of those with no signs of exclusion**

---

But what does this mean in practice? To one in 10 over-65s, it means living with constant or near constant loneliness. For the thousands who are becoming increasingly forgetful or confused, it means struggling to understand the bills, cope with paperwork or remember important family dates. For those living in unfit housing, it means spending day after day in cold, damp or unsafe conditions. To the recently bereaved, it can mean getting through an entire week without talking to a single person. For those too frail or far away to access decent public transport, it means a constant struggle to get the shopping home. Severe exclusion can mean dealing with many, or all, of these concerns at once.

Social exclusion is subjective and hard to quantify. The research findings in this report use a measure of exclusion developed by government research published in 2006, which looks at whether people are excluded

across seven dimensions of life. Although around half of people over 50 are disadvantaged in one aspect of their life, the real cause for concern is the 1.2 million over-50s facing exclusion in three or more areas of their life. These multiple, overlapping forms of disadvantage indicate 'severe exclusion', the focus of this report.

### Key facts

⇨ 1.2 million people over 50 are severely excluded: 400,000 aged 50 to 64, 360,000 aged 65 to 79, and 400,000 aged over 80. They have an average income of just £131 per week.

⇨ A woman over the age of 85 is six times more likely to be severely excluded than a woman aged between 65 and 69.

⇨ 56% of severely excluded people over 50 do not consider their health to be good, compared to just 17% of those with no signs of exclusion.

⇨ One in five people over 80 living alone are severely excluded, and men over 80 living alone are 11 times more likely to be lonely than men over 80 who are living with a partner.

⇨ The number of very old people living alone is expected to increase by 16% over the next 15 years.

⇨ Recently bereaved 65- to 79-year-olds are 10 times more likely than those who are married to be lonely; recently bereaved older people are three times more likely than married older people to show three symptoms of depression.

⇨ Over half of homes that are privately rented by the over-50s are considered non-decent. Those aged 50-64 are eight times more likely to be severely socially excluded if they rent their home privately than if they own it or pay a mortgage.

⇨ The number of people with dementia is set to rise from 700,000 at present to 1 million by 2025, significantly increasing the number at risk of social exclusion.

*15 February 2008*

⇨ The above information is reprinted with kind permission from Age Concern and is taken from their report *Out of Sight, Out of Mind*. Visit www.ageconcern.org.uk for more information or to view the full report.

*© Age Concern*

To think that when I was young I often wanted to be left alone!

# Why do we age?

### Information from Research into Ageing

*One question that has continued to preoccupy scientists and philosophers alike is why nature so cruelly discards us. Why is it that the genes we inherit from our parents do not build immortal bodies that would allow us, if not to live for ever, to live longer?*

Now the consensus among gerontologists is that since there are no evolutionary forces for selection after reproduction and parenting, it is unlikely that ageing is pre-programmed. Instead they favour the 'wear and tear' hypothesis whereby ageing is promoted by a lifetime accumulation of insidious little faults in the cells and tissues of our bodies.

How long you live ultimately comes down to a balance between how fast things go wrong with your cells and how efficiently your body works to prevent damage building up.

Dr Richard Faragher sees ageing as an accumulation of progressively worn-out parts – a bit like an old car that has developed multiple faults in several systems, such as brakes, electrics and bodywork. In his words, 'it is progressive, degenerative, universal and, sadly, irreversible'.

Life expectancies are driven by the hazards we face during our lifetime. The point is well illustrated by the different life expectancies of mammals of similar size: mice (about 2.5 years) and bats (20 years). This tells us there are no design constraints on making small mammals that live for a long time, but mice have many more predators than bats.

'So why bother,' asks Dr Faragher, 'to invest huge amounts of energy on longevity if your chances of making it through the night are fairly slim?'

Nature seems to favour those characteristics that best serve successful reproduction. In 1952 the British Nobel Laureate, Sir Peter Medawar, explained how over many generations the effects of harmful genes will accumulate after the end of the reproductive period. Medawar referred to this post-reproductive period of life as a 'genetic dustbin' where damaging and lethal genes can be expressed without penalising reproductive productivity.

Another piece of the puzzle was provided in 1957 by the evolutionary biologist George Williams, who described the concept that nature would favour the accumulation of genes that do beneficial things early in life, even though they might do harmful things later on, since most animals do not live long enough for the harmful effects to cause a problem.

In the late 1970s Research into Ageing biologist Tom Kirkwood developed the 'disposable soma theory' that neatly explains why the somatic, or non-reproductive, cells of the body are expendable.

Animals, he argues, must 'choose' whether to invest their energy into producing offspring or body maintenance. Since all living things run the risk of predators, accidents and disease, there is little point in investing much energy in repairing cells. In terms of survival of the species, resources are better employed producing offspring that perpetuate our genes.

The energy for growth and reproduction, believes Kirkwood, is made available by reducing the accuracy with which somatic cells are copied. Immortal germ cells, on the other hand, are copied, repaired and screened with a very high degree of accuracy.

In reality it all comes down to the sensible distribution of finite resources. As Kirkwood explains, 'Just as money spent on a holiday in Florida cannot be used to repair the roof, so energy spent on reproducing progeny cannot be used to repair DNA cells of the soma.'

Deterioration of our bodies after the reproductive time of our lives, which leads to ageing and ultimately death, is the price we need to pay for the immortality of our genes.

⇨ The above information is reprinted with kind permission from Research into Ageing and is taken from their document *Age of discovery: Celebrating 30 years of Research into Ageing*. Visit http://research.helptheaged.org.uk for more information or to view the full publication.

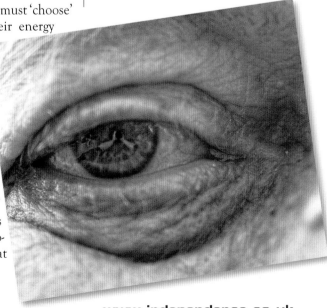

# Why do we die?

**Can genetics find a 'cure' for ageing and, therefore, dying, or will humans, like other organisms, always be at the mercy of nature? By Tim Radford**

Organisms grow old because nature doesn't need them any more. If the purpose of life is to procreate and replicate successfully – this is the logic of the so-called selfish gene theory – then it helps to stay healthy long enough to generate children and provide them with food. Immortality arrives with your offspring, and is only guaranteed when all your children also have children.

## Ageing seems inevitable but, for some scientists, it isn't obvious why this process is inexorable

Different species place their bets on life's roulette wheel in different ways. If you're an oyster or a salmon or a fruit fly, the process is over quickly enough: lay a huge number of eggs somewhere safely and die. If you're a tigress or a dolphin, the process isn't so simple: you have to bear the young, rear them, provide food on a daily basis and guide them to maturity. If you are a human, you get a little bit of extra grace: you can be useful to your grandchildren, so there is some evolutionary pressure to stay alive that little bit longer. And then there's the bonus: being human, you have all the resources of society and technology to keep you safe from predators and healthy and active for just a bit longer.

But sooner or later, the biological clock begins to run down. Cells that had faithfully renewed themselves begin to fail. A heart that pounded away in perfect synchrony begins to run down after a couple of billion beats. Joints that withstood rugby, football, rock'n'roll and the gymnasium treadmill start to creak. Skin that bloomed in the spring sunshine begins to weather and flake in life's autumn. Brains shrink, spines curve, eyes begin to fail, hearing goes, organs become cancerous, bones begin to crumble and memory perishes.

Is this going to lengthen my life, or end it I wonder?

Ageing seems inevitable but, for some scientists, it isn't obvious why this process is inexorable. Human chromosomes seem to arrive with their own lifespan timing devices called telomeres, but precisely why and how telomeres are linked to ageing is still not understood. There are genes that seem to dictate survival rates in fruit flies, nematode worms and mice, and these genes almost certainly exist in humans, but what works in an insect or even another mammal may not be much help to a human anxious to hang around a bit longer. Even so, in the last half of the 20th century, life expectancies were increasing everywhere in the developed and developing world, wherever there was appropriate sanitation, nutrition, education and medical care; and small groups of scientists had begun to ask whether life could be extended indefinitely.

### Clues to survival

A much larger group was prepared to ask a simpler question: could a healthy, active, enjoyable life be extended a bit longer? Quite how this can be done – in the individuals or in society as a whole – is not so easily answered, but epidemiological and biochemical research has begun to produce some clues to survival. These are, in no particular order:

Be at the top. Research in Japan, the US and Britain has confirmed that social status is linked to health and lifespan. Top civil servants outlive their deputies. Oscar-winning film stars on average live four years longer than ordinary Hollywood actors. The same is true for queen bees, which live 10 times longer than worker bees.

Be British. Better still, be Japanese. British people in the more comfortable echelons of society tend to have lower rates of diabetes, hypertension, heart disease, stroke, lung disease and cancer than their American counterparts, even though they spend less on healthcare. The Japanese, of course, do even better.

Choose your ancestors carefully: There are genes that control ageing. Nobody knows exactly what they are or how they work, but you stand a much better chance of being a centenarian if you have a sibling who has made it to 100. Exceptional longevity runs in families. So it is part of inheritance.

Eat wisely: Forget about superfoods, but watch what you eat. Rats, mice and other creatures with restricted calorie intakes survive longer than their sated siblings. What works for mice may not work for humans, but there is no doubt that overeating multiplies health hazards.

*29 April 2008*

© *Guardian Newspapers Limited 2008*

# Lounging around could speed up ageing process

**Following a couch potato lifestyle could leave you 10 years biologically older than your more active peers, according to research published in the journal *Archives of Internal Medicine***

It's already well known that regular exercise helps to cut the risk of many diseases including heart disease, cancer and diabetes. But this new research is the first to suggest that keeping fit can have an effect on the ageing process too.

A team of scientists at King's College London studied 2,401 twins who were asked detailed questions about their lifestyles. These included how much exercise they did and whether or not they smoked. The team then took blood samples in order to analyse their DNA.

> **'Inactivity may diminish life expectancy not only by predisposing to ageing-related diseases but also because it may influence the ageing process itself'**

The researchers were particularly interested in the length of special chain-like structures called telomeres – which protect DNA on chromosomes. These get shorter as we get older and are thought to be a good marker of the biological age of a person. The team found that the participants who were less physically active had shorter telomeres than people who were fit. In fact the results showed that there was a difference of about 10 years of ageing between the most active and the least active volunteers. When the researchers compared twins who had different levels of physical activity, they found similar results.

Exercise bestowed the same anti-ageing benefits even when other factors were taken into account such as weight, smoking and socio-economic status.

'Inactivity may diminish life expectancy not only by predisposing to ageing-related diseases but also because it may influence the ageing process itself,' reported the team.

So why does keeping fit keep you young? The scientists believe that people who do little exercise are more exposed to oxidative stress, which damages cells. Exercise also helps to relieve psychological stress which is known to hasten the ageing process.

'Guidelines recommend that 30 minutes of moderate-intensity physical activity at least five days a week can have significant health benefits,' the authors write. 'Our results underscore the vital importance of these guidelines. They show that adults who partake in regular physical activity are biologically younger than sedentary individuals. This conclusion provides a powerful message that could be used by clinicians to promote the potential anti-ageing effect of regular exercise.'

'We would encourage everyone to take responsibility for their own fitness,' says Katherine Murphy, spokesperson for the Patients Association. 'However, the government should do more to promote exercise as part of a healthy lifestyle.'

⇨ The above information is reprinted with kind permission from Saga. Visit www.saga.co.uk for more information.

© Saga

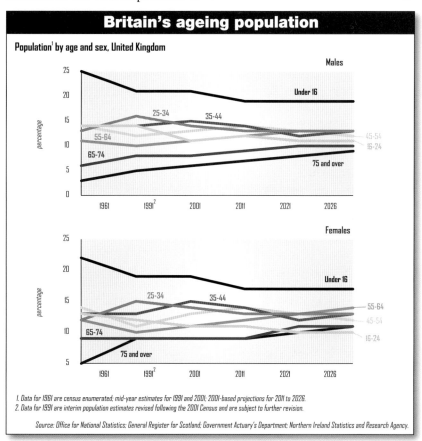

**Britain's ageing population**

Population¹ by age and sex, United Kingdom

*Males*

Under 16 · 25-34 · 35-44 · 55-64 · 65-74 · 45-54 · 16-24 · 75 and over

1961 · 1991² · 2001 · 2011 · 2021 · 2026

*Females*

Under 16 · 25-34 · 35-44 · 55-64 · 45-54 · 65-74 · 16-24 · 75 and over

1961 · 1991² · 2001 · 2011 · 2021 · 2026

1. Data for 1961 are census enumerated; mid-year estimates for 1991 and 2001; 2001-based projections for 2011 to 2026.
2. Data for 1991 are interim population estimates revised following the 2001 Census and are subject to further revision.

Source: Office for National Statistics; General Register for Scotland; Government Actuary's Department; Northern Ireland Statistics and Research Agency.

# Increasing life expectancy

## Lifestyle changes increase life expectancy 14 years

Four behaviours which can add an average of 14 years' life expectancy have been identified in a study led by Cambridge University.

The research, spearheaded by Dr Kay-Tee Khaw at Cambridge's Institute of Public Health, found that those who exercised regularly, ate five portions of fruit and vegetables a day, didn't smoke, and had a moderate alcohol consumption lived an average of 14 years longer than those who adopted none of these behaviours.

The study's results are particularly important given the ageing population of many European nations, including the UK. All four factors are achievable lifestyle changes which can improve quality of life for middle-aged and older people.

20,000 men and women aged 45-79 took part in the study. Between 1993 and 1997 they completed a questionnaire, which awarded them a score between 0 and 4.

A point was awarded for not smoking, an alcohol intake of between 1 and 14 units per week, a level of Vitamin C in the blood consistent with eating five portions of fruit and vegetables a day, and not being physically inactive. Physical inactivity was defined as having a sedentary job and not taking any form of exercise in leisure time. Deaths were then recorded in the subject group till 2006.

After taking account of the influence of age, the researchers found that, over the course of 11 years, those who had a score of zero were four times more likely to die than those with a score of four.

They also found that those scoring zero had the same risk of dying as those who were 14 years older than them but scored four in the questionnaire. Both of these findings were independent of social class or Body Mass Index.

The Cambridge study, which is part of the European Prospective Investigation into Cancer and Nutrition, is unusual in focusing on the combined impact of these activities. Whilst there is a great deal of evidence about the impact on health and life expectancy of these factors singly, very little research has been conducted on their combined effect.

The study, titled *Combined Impact of Health Behaviours and Mortality in Men and Women: The EPIC-Norfolk Prospective Population Study*, has been published by the Public Library of Science's journal *PLoS Medicine*.

An accompanying editorial addresses the issues involved for individuals trying to make these lifestyle changes, and the complex processes by which research becomes public policy.

*By Tom Russell, University of Cambridge Communications Office.*

*8 January 2008*

⇨ The above information is reprinted with kind permission from the University of Cambridge. Visit www.cam.ac.uk for more information.

© University of Cambridge

## Life expectancy and healthy ageing

### Highlights from the Office for National Statistics

In recent years, Parliament has passed legislation raising the State Pension Age (SPA). Women's SPA will rise from 60 to 65 years between 2010 and 2020; then SPA for both sexes will rise to 68 by 2046.

In coming years, as life expectancies continue rising, the life expectancy gap between the sexes at SPA will narrow; and life expectancies at SPA will stabilise from 2021. Period life expectancy projections give women around 23 years of life expectancy at SPA in 2021 to 2051, compared with around 21 years for men.

This chapter looks at whether longer life expectancy is associated with longer 'health expectancy' in old age, allowing people to enjoy their retirement in good health. In 2004, men at age 65 had 16.6 years of life expectancy and 12.5 years' healthy life expectancy, compared with 19.4 and 14.5 years respectively for women.

However, increases in healthy life expectancy between 1981 and 2001 were smaller than increases in life expectancy. If this trend continues, then as SPA rises, people will spend a greater part of their retirement in poor health.

There are inequalities in life expectancy estimates between social class groups based on occupation. If the current trends continue, those from the lowest social class groups may experience declining life expectancy at SPA in 2021 to 2051.

In 2003, life expectancy for men and women at ages 60 and 65 was highest in England and lowest in Scotland. There were also differences in healthy life expectancy and disability-free life expectancy of people living in different parts of the UK. If these inequalities persist, the effects of a future rise in SPA in the UK as a whole will be felt differently by pensioners in different parts of the UK.

*17 January 2008*

⇨ The above information is reprinted with kind permission from the Office for National Statistics. Visit www.statistics.gov.uk for more information.

© Crown copyright

# What is dementia?

## Information from the Alzheimer's Society

**D**ementia describes different brain disorders that trigger a loss of brain function. These conditions are all usually progressive and eventually severe.

There are more than 100 different types of dementia. Alzheimer's disease is the most common type, affecting 62 per cent of those diagnosed, almost 417,000 people.

Other types of dementia include: vascular dementia affecting 17 per cent of those diagnosed and mixed dementia affecting 10 per cent of those diagnosed.

## One in three older people will end their lives with a form of dementia

Symptoms of dementia include memory loss, confusion and problems with speech and understanding. Dementia is a terminal condition.

### Who is affected?

There are 700,000 people with dementia in the UK. This will rise to over 1 million people by 2025 and 1.7 million by 2051.

There are 575,000 people with dementia in England. The condition affects more than 56,000 people in Scotland, 16,000 in Northern Ireland and more than 36,000 people in Wales.

One person in every 14, aged over 65, in the UK has dementia. This rises to one in six people over 80. One in three older people will end their lives with a form of dementia

More than 60 per cent of all care home residents, aged over 65, have a form of dementia.

More than 15,000 people under 65 have dementia in the UK.

Dementia affects 11,000 people from black and minority ethnic groups in the UK.

### How much does it cost?

Dementia costs the country £17 billion every year or £539 a second.

Unpaid carers supporting someone with dementia save the economy £6 billion a year.

Two-thirds of people with late onset dementia live at home, meaning families bear the biggest burden.

### How does the UK compare to other countries?

More than 24 million people have dementia today with the numbers affected doubling every 20 years to more than 80 million by 2040.

Another 4.6 million people will develop dementia around the world this year.

### What about treatments and research?

There is no cure for Alzheimer's disease or any other type of dementia. Delaying the onset of dementia by five years would halve the number of deaths from the condition, saving 30,000 lives a year.

Just two per cent of government funding through the Medical Research Council was spent on dementia research in 2003/4.

Of the 32 million spent on mental health research by the MRC in 2003/04, just £7.2m funded dementia research.

Just £11 is spent on research into dementia, per person living with the condition, in the UK compared, with £105 in America.

### Where can you go for advice and information?

Call the Alzheimer's Society helpline on 0845 300 0336 or visit the website http://www.alzheimers.org.uk/

⇨ The above information is reprinted with kind permission from the Alzheimer's Society, accessed on 2 July 2008. Visit www.alzheimers.org.uk for more information.

© *Alzheimer's Society*

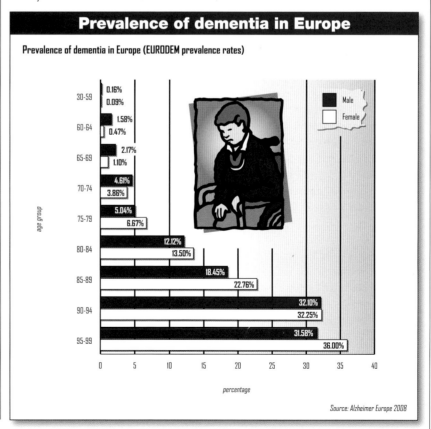

**Prevalence of dementia in Europe**

Prevalence of dementia in Europe (EURODEM prevalence rates)

| age group | Male | Female |
|---|---|---|
| 30-59 | 0.16% | 0.09% |
| 60-64 | 1.58% | 0.47% |
| 65-69 | 2.17% | 1.10% |
| 70-74 | 4.61% | 3.86% |
| 75-79 | 5.04% | 6.67% |
| 80-84 | 12.12% | 13.50% |
| 85-89 | 18.45% | 22.76% |
| 90-94 | 32.10% | 32.25% |
| 95-99 | 31.58% | 36.00% |

percentage

Source: Alzheimer Europe 2008

# Who is affected by Alzheimer's disease?

## Information from Alzheimer Europe

On the basis of comparisons of large groups of people with Alzheimer's disease with others who have not been affected, researchers suggest that there are a number of risk factors. This means that some people are more likely to suffer from the disease than others. However, it is unlikely that the disease could be traced to a single cause. It is more likely that a combination of factors lead to its development, with the importance of particular factors differing from one person to another.

### Age

About one person out of twenty over the age of 65 suffers from Alzheimer's disease and less than one person in a thousand under the age of 65. However, it is important to note that although people do tend to become forgetful as time goes on, the vast majority of people over 80 stay mentally alert. This means that although the likelihood of suffering from Alzheimer's disease increases with age, old age does not itself cause the disease. Nevertheless, recent evidence suggests that age-related problems such as arteriosclerosis may be important contributing factors. Also, as people are now living longer than in the past, the number of people with Alzheimer's disease and other forms of dementia will most probably increase.

### Sex

Some studies have suggested that more women are affected by the disease than men at any one time. However, this can be misleading because women as a group live longer than men. This means that if men were to live as long as women and did not die of other illnesses, the number suffering from Alzheimer's disease would be about the same as that for women.

### Genetic factors (heredity)

In an extremely limited number of families Alzheimer's disease is a dominant genetic disorder. Members of such families inherit from one of their parents the part of the DNA (the genetic make-up), which causes the disease. On average, half the children of an affected parent will develop the disease. For the members of such families who develop Alzheimer's disease, the age of onset tends to be relatively low, usually between 35 and 60. The onset is fairly constant within the family. A link between chromosome 21 and Alzheimer's disease has been discovered. As Down's syndrome is caused by an anomaly in this chromosome, many children with Down's syndrome will develop Alzheimer's disease if they reach middle age, although they may not display the full range of symptoms.

---

**Although the likelihood of suffering from Alzheimer's disease increases with age, old age does not itself cause the disease**

---

### Head injury

There is evidence to suggest that a person who has received a severe blow to the head may be at risk of developing Alzheimer's disease. This risk is higher if at the time of the injury the person is over 50, has a specific gene (apoE4) and lost consciousness just after the accident.

### Other factors

There is no conclusive evidence to suggest that any particular group of people is more or less likely to develop Alzheimer's disease. Race, profession, geographical and socio-economic situation are not determinants of the disease. However, there is mounting evidence to suggest that people with a higher level of education are at less risk than those with a lower level of education.

⇨ The above information is reprinted with kind permission from Alzheimer Europe. Visit www.alzheimer-europe.org for more information.

© *Alzheimer Europe*

# Reversing the signs of Alzheimer's

## Scottish scientists are one step further to finding a cure for Alzheimer's, thanks to the development of a compound which reverses signs of the disease

The biologists at the University of St Andrews have developed man-made compounds capable of blocking a nerve cell interaction known to lead to the symptoms of the disease. The researchers have shown that it is possible to reverse some of the signs associated with Alzheimer's.

Dr Frank Gunn-Moore's team, in collaboration with researchers in the US, have successfully reversed a sign for the progression of the disease and prevented the death of brain cells. This subsequently leads to improved memory and learning ability that was already damaged.

The results of the recent study – carried out in the lab using a model of the disease – has been described as 'exciting' by the Alzheimer's Research Trust, who helped to fund the research.

Alzheimer's affects around half a million people in the UK – a number which is expected to double with the general ageing of the population over the next generation. The discovery that Alzheimer's is caused by a toxic protein which kills off nerve cells in the brains of sufferers, has led to the search for a compound which can block or reduce the debilitating interaction.

Alzheimer's is linked to the build-up of amyloid protein which eventually forms 'senile plaques'. The amyloid protein inflicts damage by interacting with an enzyme called ABAD (Amyloid Beta Alcohol Dehydrogenase) and releasing toxic substances which kill brain cells.

Dr Gunn-Moore's research initially focussed on developing the three-dimensional shape of ABAD and understanding how amyloid attaches itself to the structure.

Dr Gunn-Moore, a senior lecturer at the University's School of Biology, said, 'Alzheimer's sufferers produce too much amyloid and ABAD in their brains. Based on our knowledge of ABAD, we produced an inhibitor that can prevent amyloid attaching to it in a living model. We have shown that it is possible to reverse some of the signs associated with Alzheimer's disease.

---

**Alzheimer's affects around half a million people in the UK – a number which is expected to double with the general ageing of the population over the next generation**

---

'The work is now being continued to try and refine the inhibitor into a potential drug. Our research holds a possible key for the treatment of Alzheimer's disease, particularly in its early stages.'

In Alzheimer's the protein ABAD is targeted by the toxic substance amyloid which leads to the death of nerve cells.

The Alzheimer's Research Trust have awarded the St Andrews team a further grant to develop the research over the next three years – the funding will allow PhD researcher Kirsty Muirhead to build on the success of recent results. Kirsty aims to find and test other compounds in order to find the inhibitor with the greatest potential for use in future therapies.

Rebecca Wood, Chief Executive of the Alzheimer's Research Trust, said, 'A drug that can stop Alzheimer's disease from killing brain cells is a holy grail for researchers working to overcome the devastating condition which affects more than 500,000 people in the UK. We wish Dr Gunn-Moore and his team well in this exciting research.'
*23 July 2007*

⇨ The above information is reprinted with kind permission from the University of St Andrews. Visit www.st-andrews.ac.uk for more information.

# Alzheimer's disease to quadruple by 2050

## More than 26 million now estimated to have the disease worldwide

More than 26 million people worldwide were estimated to be living with Alzheimer's disease in 2006, according to a study led by researchers at the Johns Hopkins Bloomberg School of Public Health. The researchers also concluded the global prevalence of Alzheimer's disease will grow to more than 106 million by 2050. By that time, 43 per cent of those with Alzheimer's disease will need high-level care, equivalent to that of a nursing home. The findings were presented on June 10 at the Second Alzheimer's Association International Conference on Prevention of Dementia held in Washington, DC and are published in the Association's journal, *Alzheimer's & Dementia*.

---

## More than 26 million people worldwide were estimated to be living with Alzheimer's disease in 2006

---

'We face a looming global epidemic of Alzheimer's disease as the world's population ages,' said the study's lead author, Ron Brookmeyer, PhD, professor in Biostatistics and chair of the Master of Public Health Programme at the Bloomberg School of Public Health. 'By 2050, 1 in 85 persons worldwide will have Alzheimer's disease. However, if we can make even modest advances in preventing Alzheimer's disease or delay its progression, we could have a huge global public health impact.'

According to Brookmeyer and his co-authors, interventions that could delay the onset of Alzheimer's disease by as little as one year would reduce prevalence of the disease by 12 million

fewer cases in 2050. A similar delay in both the onset and progression of Alzheimer's disease would result in a smaller overall reduction of 9.2 million cases by 2050, because slower disease progression would mean more people surviving with early-stage disease symptoms. However, nearly all of that decline would be attributable to decreases in those needing costly late-stage disease treatment in 2050.

The largest increase in the prevalence of Alzheimer's will occur in Asia, where 48 per cent of the world's Alzheimer's cases currently reside. The number of Alzheimer's cases is expected to grow in Asia from 12.65 million in 2006 to 62.85 million in 2050; at that time, 59 per cent of the world's Alzheimer's cases will live in Asia.

To forecast the worldwide prevalence of Alzheimer's disease, the researcher created a multi-state mathematical computer model using United Nations population projections and other data on the incidence and mortality of Alzheimer's.

The research was funded by Elan Pharmaceuticals and Wyeth Pharmaceuticals.

Additional authors of the article 'Forecasting the global burden of Alzheimer's disease' include Elizabeth Johnson of the Johns Hopkins Bloomberg School of Public Health, Kathryn Zieger-Graham with St Olaf College and H. Michael Arrighi with Elan Pharmaceuticals.

*10 June 2007*

⇨ The above information is re-printed with kind permission from Johns Hopkins Bloomberg School of Public Health. Visit www.jhsph.edu for more information.

*© Johns Hopkins Bloomberg School of Public Health*

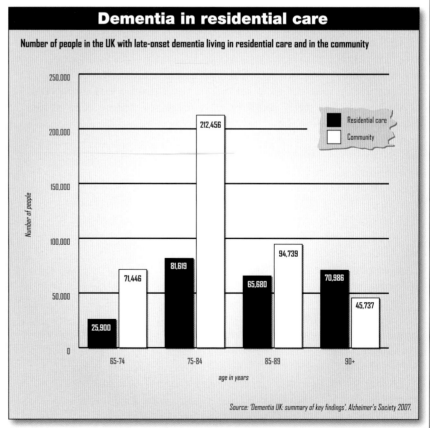

**Dementia in residential care**

Number of people in the UK with late-onset dementia living in residential care and in the community

Legend: ■ Residential care □ Community

| age in years | Residential care | Community |
| --- | --- | --- |
| 65-74 | 25,900 | 71,446 |
| 75-84 | 81,619 | 212,456 |
| 85-89 | 65,680 | 94,739 |
| 90+ | 70,986 | 45,737 |

Number of people (y-axis): 0 to 250,000

Source: 'Dementia UK: summary of key findings'. Alzheimer's Society 2007.

# Fear of dementia

## Brits fear dementia more than other conditions

**B**ritons are worried about heart disease and stroke, but they downright dread dementia, an Alzheimer's Research Trust survey has found.

The YouGov poll, commissioned by the Alzheimer's Research Trust, revealed that 26% of people are more concerned about getting dementia than any other health condition. Only fear of cancer is greater (41%).

Among over-55s, fear of dementia actually supersedes fear of cancer; 39% of over-55s are most concerned about dementia, compared to 30% who are more scared of cancer.

---

**Britons are worried about heart disease and stroke, but they downright dread dementia, an Alzheimer's Research Trust survey has found**

---

This appears to reflect the comments of Terry Pratchett, the best-selling author and Patron of the Alzheimer's Research Trust, who caused a media furore in March when he said:

'I'd like a chance to die like my father did – of cancer, at 86. Remember, I'm speaking as a man with Alzheimer's, which strips away your living self a bit at a time. Before he went to spend his last two weeks in a hospice he was bustling around the house, fixing things. He talked to us right up to the last few days, knowing who we were and who he was. Right now, I envy him.'

Rebecca Wood, Chief Executive of the Alzheimer's Research Trust, said:

'It is easy to see why people are so scared of Alzheimer's and other dementias, as this YouGov poll shows. 25 million people in the UK know someone with dementia, and 700,000 people have the condition, a number expected to double within a generation. It is a nasty disease that we must do everything possible to tackle. Research into treatments and a possible cure is still terribly underfunded. Cancer, quite justly, receives substantial government funding for medical research; dementia should be treated proportionately too.'

Care costs for dementia are around £17 billion per year: more than cancer, stroke and heart disease combined.

Only £11 is spent on research into Alzheimer's for every person affected by the disease, compared with £289 for cancer patients. 82% of the public support an increase in dementia research funding.
*26 May 2008*

⇨ The above information is reprinted with kind permission from the Alzheimers Research Trust. Visit www.alzheimers-research.org.uk for more information.

*© Alzheimer's Research Trust*

# Seniors playground swings into action

## The first playground in the UK aimed specifically at older people has opened in Manchester

**T**he 'Older People's Play Area' cost £15,000 to build and features 6 pieces of fitness equipment intended to provide gentle exercise for the over-60s.

Members of the local resident's association (DAMRA) on the Dam Head Estate in Blackley started the project after being inspired by a similar play area in Germany.

'It's brilliant,' says Louise Huntington, spokesperson for Northwards Housing who funded the project. 'The idea is to bring the community together and encourage older people to exercise and have fun at the same time. The equipment is very gentle and it's just next to a children's playground so grandparents can nip over while the grandchildren are playing next door.'

Each piece of equipment has been designed to exercise a different part of the body. There is a skate machine to train the leg muscles and another based on skiing which is used to strengthen the hips. All the machines are simple to use and low impact so there is little chance of anyone sustaining an injury. Some parts of the stations are accessible to wheelchair users.

Joan Fitzgerald, 76, chairperson of DAMRA and the driving force behind the project, was one of the first to try out the new playground. 'It's great,' she said, 'I went with a whole crowd of older people and we never stopped giggling. Too many people our age spend too much time indoors. This is a great way to meet people and get a bit of exercise at the same time.'

Joan hopes that people all over the country will take up the idea and we will see 'Older People's Play Areas' springing up throughout the UK.

⇨ The above information is reprinted with kind permission from Saga. Visit www.saga.co.uk for more information.

*© Saga*

⇨ There are nearly 12 million pensioners, almost one in five of the UK's total population. (page 3)

⇨ Current life expectancy aged 65 is 84.7 for women and 81.9 for men. At birth, they are 81.3 and 76.9 respectively. (page 3)

⇨ 73% of older people in Great Britain agree that age discrimination exists in the daily lives of older people. (page 4)

⇨ In 1950, 8 out of every 100 people were over 60. By 2050, 22 out of every 100 people will be over 60. (page 5)

⇨ Ageing is a global phenomenon. The world's elderly population – people 60 years of age and older – is the fastest growing age group. By 2050 about 80% of the elderly will be living in developing countries. (page 6)

⇨ Ipsos MORI's data shows that most older people are politically literate and socially engaged. The older age groups are far more likely to vote than younger people, indeed a quarter of the voters at the 2005 general election were aged 65+, and more than two in five were aged 55 or over. (page 7)

⇨ 86% of Brits know it's illegal to discriminate on age at work. But 16 million workers have witnessed ageist practices at work in the last year alone. (page 11)

⇨ Birmingham Midshires' 'Life 2' campaign, which explores the issues affecting the lifestyle of the over-55s, reveals that just three per cent of people in this age group have suffered age discrimination at work, compared to 11 per cent of young people aged 18 to 24. (page 12)

⇨ Less than half of Britons chose the word 'happy' to describe how they felt on the first day of retirement, evidence the traditional sudden stop approach no longer works for many people. (page 15)

⇨ 4% or 342,400 elderly people were neglected or abused in the last year by family, close friends and care workers, neighbours and acquaintances. (page 18)

⇨ Successive generations of retirees have increased their consumption of goods with, for example, later generations spending more on leisure activities such as holidays. (page 19)

⇨ More than half of survey respondents (55 per cent) in their early 50s are still working the nine-to-five grind, whilst 23 per cent of those aged over 55 have given up full-time work. (page 20)

⇨ Far from retiring quietly, young people today expect to be able to afford the things they enjoy now when they retire with foreign holidays, satellite TV and gym membership as standard. With over half the nation's under 34-year-olds not saving anything at all, they are at risk of becoming the 'big dreams, small assets' generation. (page 21)

⇨ Britain's pension crisis is set to escalate, a study has warned, with a generation of adults facing the triple pressure of the financial 'hat trick' scenario of supporting both their parents and their own children, whilst having no financial plans to safeguard their own future either. (page 22)

⇨ The UK's state pension system was rated the worst in Europe for the second year running in a report published in November 2007. (page 25)

⇨ Rising care charges are putting older and disabled people at risk of not being able to afford to eat, heat their homes, wash or get essential support, says a report. (page 26)

⇨ Eight out of ten people in Britain are very concerned about the quality of care they or their loved ones will get in later life, research for Age Concern has revealed. (page 28)

⇨ More than a third (37 per cent) of British adults over 50 have had to put someone into residential care. (page 29)

⇨ 1.2 million people over 50 are severely excluded: 400,000 aged 50 to 64, 360,000 aged 65 to 79, and 400,000 aged over 80. They have an average income of just £131 per week. (page 30)

⇨ There are inequalities in life expectancy estimates between social class groups based on occupation. If the current trends continue, those from the lowest social class groups may experience declining life expectancy at State Pension Age in 2021 to 2051. (page 34)

⇨ There are 700,000 people with dementia in the UK. This will rise to over 1 million people by 2025 and 1.7 million by 2051. (page 35)

⇨ More than 24 million people have dementia in the world today with the numbers affected doubling every 20 years to more than 80 million by 2040. (page 35)

⇨ About one person out of twenty over the age of 65 suffers from Alzheimer's disease and less than one person in a thousand under the age of 65. However, it is important to note that although people do tend to become forgetful as time goes on, the vast majority of people over 80 stay mentally alert. (page 36)

# GLOSSARY

**Ageing**
The process of growing older.

**Age discrimination**
Treating someone unfavourably because of their age.

**Alzheimer's disease**
The most common form of dementia. Alzheimer's is a progressive disease involving the degeneration of parts of the brain, causing memory loss, and there is no known cure.

**Dementia**
A progressive deterioration of mental powers and memory. Dementia usually affects older people and the likelihood of developing it increases with age. There is no cure for most types of dementia. Alzheimer's is the most common and most well-known form of dementia.

**Elder abuse**
Mistreatment of a vulnerable older person, most often by a carer or family member, causing them harm and distress.

**Fuel poverty**
The inability to afford adequate heating.

**Life expectancy**
The average life span of a population. Life expectancy varies according to gender, lifestyle and the area a person lives in. The average life expectancy within the UK is 79 years.

**Means-tested**
Entitlement to benefits from the government based on one's income.

**Pension**
Regular payment to an individual after retirement.

**Pensions Act 2007**
This act introduced reforms to the state pension. The number of years during which contributions need to be made in order to receive a full Basic State Pension on retirement will be reduced to 30 years from April 6, 2010 and the State Pension Age will gradually increase to 68 for men and women.

**Poverty line**
The minimum level of income needed for an adequate standard of living. People living on an income below this level are said to be below the poverty line.

**Retirement**
Ceasing to work, usually due to age. Most people will retire when they reach State Pension Age, but this varies from person to person.

**State Pension Age (SPA)**
The State Pension Age or SPA in the UK is 65 for men and 60 for women. On reaching SPA, individuals are entitled to a state pension if they leave employment, the value of which will depend upon contributions made during the individual's working life. Under the terms of the Pensions Act 2007, the SPA will gradually rise to 68 for both men and women.

# INDEX

age discrimination  4, 8-13
  young people  12
ageing
  attitudes to  14-15
  effect of exercise  33
  and health  31-9
  effect of lifestyle  33, 34
ageing population
  global  5, 6
  UK  3
ageing process  1-2, 31-2
Alzheimer's disease 4, 36-9
Amyloid Beta Alcohol Dehydrogenase (ABAD)  37
arthritis  4

Basic State Pension  3, 23

care homes  27-8
care services  4
  concerns about  28
  funding  29
  rising costs  26
carers, older people as  4, 5
cell ageing  1
consumption patterns, older people  19
costs
  of ageing  19-30
  dementia  35
  home care  26
crime, fear of  3

deaths, older people  4
dementia  4, 35-9
  fear of  39
Denmark, state pension  25
developing countries
  ageing population  5
  pensions  24
disaster victims, older people  6

elder abuse  4, 6, 16-18
employment
  and age discrimination 8-13
  past retirement age  10, 15
exercise
  effect on ageing process  2, 33
  older people  39

falls, older people  4, 6
family abuse of older people  17
financial abuse  16
financial freedom, older people  20
financial planning for old age  21-2
fitness, effect on ageing process  33, 34
fitness equipment for older people  39

fuel poverty  3

gender and Alzheimer's disease  36
genetic factors
  and ageing  2, 32
  and Alzheimer's disease  36

head injury and Alzheimer's disease  36
health, older people  4, 6, 8
health care  6
  see also care services
health inequalities  6
healthy ageing  34
heredity and Alzheimer's disease  36
HIV/AIDS sufferers, older people as carers  5
home care services  4
  costs  26
homelessness and housing, older people  4

income, pensioners  3
incontinence  4
isolation  3, 8, 17, 30

legislation, age discrimination  10, 11
leisure, older people  3,  8
life expectancy  6
  increasing  32-4
  UK  3, 34
lifestyle and ageing  2, 34
loneliness  3, 8, 17, 30
long-term illness  4

mental health, older people  4

National Health Service and older people  4
neglect  17
nutrition and ageing  2

objective justification, age discrimination  9
older people
  as carers  4, 5
  health  4, 6, 8, 35-9
  spending  19
  working  10, 15
  worldwide  5, 6
  UK  3-4, 7-8

pay gap  13
pensions
  Europe  25
  saving for  21, 22
  UK  3, 23, 25
  universal social pension  24
Pensions Act  23
physical abuse  16

playground for older people  39
political engagement, older people  7
population ageing
    global  6
    UK  3
positive action and age discrimination  9-10
poverty, older people  3
psychological abuse  16

retired people
    spending patterns  19
    working  10, 15
retirement
    feelings about  15
    saving for  21, 22
    working after retirement age  10, 15

saving for old age  21, 22
sensory impairment  4
sexual abuse  16-17
social exclusion, older people  30

social status and ageing  32
spending patterns, older people  19
state pensions *see* pensions
strokes  4

telomeres  32, 33
training and age discrimination  9

universal social pension  24

vocational training and age discrimination  9

winter deaths  4
women and ageing population  5
working past retirement age  10, 15
workplace age discrimination  8-13

young people
    age discrimination  12
    failing to save for old age  21

# Additional Resources

*Other* Issues *titles*

If you are interested in researching further some of the issues raised in *An Ageing Population*, you may like to read the following titles in the **Issues** series:

⇨ Vol. 162 *Staying Fit* (ISBN 978 1 86168 455 4)

⇨ Vol. 160 *Poverty and Exclusion* (ISBN 978 1 86168 453 0)

⇨ Vol. 154 *The Gender Gap* (ISBN 978 1 86168 441 7)

⇨ Vol. 152 *Euthanasia and the Right to Die* (ISBN 978 1 86168 439 4)

⇨ Vol. 150 *Migration and Population* (ISBN 978 1 86168 423 3)

⇨ Vol. 141 *Mental Health* (ISBN 978 1 86168 407 3)

⇨ Vol. 135 *Coping with Disability* (ISBN 978 1 86168 387 8)

⇨ Vol. 116 *Grief and Loss* (ISBN 978 1 86168 349 6)

⇨ Vol. 107 *Work Issues* (ISBN 978 1 86168 327 4)

For more information about these titles, visit our website at www.independence.co.uk/publicationslist

*Useful organisations*

You may find the websites of the following organisations useful for further research:

⇨ **Alzheimer Europe:** www.alzheimer-europe.org

⇨ **Alzheimers Research Trust:** www.alzheimers-research.org.uk

⇨ **Alzheimer's Society:** www.alzheimers.org.uk

⇨ **Age Concern:** www.ageconcern.org.uk

⇨ **The Age and Employment Network:** www.taen.org.uk

⇨ **Carers UK:** www.carersuk.org

⇨ **Department for Work and Pensions:** www.dwp.gov.uk

⇨ **Department of Health:** www.dh.gov.uk

⇨ **Employers Forum on Age:** www.efa.org.uk

⇨ **Equality and Human Rights Commission:** www.equalityhumanrights.com

⇨ **Guide2care:** www.guide2care.com

⇨ **HelpAge International:** www.helpage.org

⇨ **Help the Aged:** www.helptheaged.org.uk

⇨ **The Naked Scientists:** www.thenakedscientists.com

⇨ **Saga:** www.saga.co.uk

⇨ **World Health Organisation:** www.who.int

# ACKNOWLEDGEMENTS

The publisher is grateful for permission to reproduce the following material.

While every care has been taken to trace and acknowledge copyright, the publisher tenders its apology for any accidental infringement or where copyright has proved untraceable. The publisher would be pleased to come to a suitable arrangement in any such case with the rightful owner.

## Chapter One: Ageing Trends
*The ageing process*, © Guide2care, *What is ageing?*, © The Naked Scientists, *Older people in the UK*, © Help the Aged, *Facts and figures: global ageing*, © HelpAge International, *10 facts on ageing and the life course*, © World Health Organisation, *Profile of the UK's older people*, © Ipsos MORI, *Age discrimination*, © Equality and Human Rights Commission, *Number of working pensioners continues to rise*, © The Age and Employment Network, *Knowledge of age laws increasing*, © Employers Forum on Age, *Work experienced*, © Birmingham Midshires, *Plans to outlaw age discrimination announced*, © politics.co.uk, *Ignoring old age won't keep you young*, © Telegraph Group Ltd, *Reinventing the retirement cliff edge*, © Crown copyright is reproduced with the permission of Her Majesty's Stationery Office, *Dignified conclusions*, © Guardian Newspapers Ltd, *Loneliness a major worry*, © Saga, *Prevalence of elder abuse*, © Crown copyright is reproduced with the permission of Her Majesty's Stationery Office.

## Chapter Two: The Cost of Ageing
*Retirees spending freely*, © Economic and Social Research Council, *Life begins at 55*, © Birmingham Midshires, *Aim high, save low*, © Crown copyright is reproduced with the permission of Her Majesty's Stationery Office, *Next generation of Brits facing bleak future*, © Norwich Union, *Pensions Act 2007*, © Crown copyright is reproduced with the permission of Her Majesty's Stationery Office, *Pension could protect world's poorest*, © HelpAge International, *UK state pensions is 'worst in Europe'*, © Guardian Newspapers Ltd, *Charging into poverty*, © Carers UK, *Care homes*, © Help the Aged, *Huge public worries about quality of care*, ©

Age Concern, *Funding long-term care*, © Partnership, *Out of sight, out of mind*, © Age Concern.

## Chapter Three: Ageing and Health
*Why do we age?*, © Help the Aged, *Why do we die?*, © Guardian Newspapers Ltd, *Lounging around could speed up ageing process*, © Saga, *Increasing life expectancy*, © University of Cambridge, *Life expectancy and healthy ageing*, © Crown copyright is reproduced with the permission of Her Majesty's Stationery Office, *What is dementia?*, © Alzheimer's Society, *Who is affected by Alzheimer's disease?*, © Alzheimer Europe, *Reversing the signs of Alzheimer's*, © University of St Andrews, *Alzheimer's disease to quadruple by 2050*, © Johns Hopkins Bloomberg School of Public Health, *Fear of dementia*, © Alzheimer's Research Trust, *Seniors playground swings into action*, © Saga.

## Photographs
**Flickr:** pages 5 (Jessie Reeder); 19 (Michelle Hofstrand); 29 (Marina Guimarães); 31 (Randen Pederson).
**Stock Xchng:** pages 11 (Faakhir Rizvi); 13, 14 (Melodi T); 22 (Marcelo Moura).

## Illustrations
Pages 2, 24, 27, 37: Simon Kneebone; pages 7, 18: Bev Aisbett; pages 9, 25, 30, 32: Don Hatcher; pages 12, 26, 36: Angelo Madrid.

Additional editorial by Claire Owen, on behalf of Independence Educational Publishers.

And with thanks to the team: Mary Chapman, Sandra Dennis, Claire Owen and Jan Sunderland.

Lisa Firth
Cambridge
September, 2008